TEXT AND INTERPRETATION

JOB

A Practical Commentary

A. van Selms

Translated by John Vriend

GRAND RAPIDS, MICHIGAN
WILLIAM B. EERDMANS PUBLISHING COMPANY

Copyright © 1985 by William B. Eerdmans Publishing Company
255 Jefferson Ave. S.E., Grand Rapids, Mich. 49503

Translated from the Dutch edition *Job: Een praktische bijbelverklaring*, part
of the Tekst en Toelichting series. © Uitgeversmaatschappij J. H. Kok—
Kampen, 1984.

Library of Congress Cataloging in Publication Data

Selms, A. van (Adrianus), 1906-
  Job.

  (Text and interpretation)
  Translation of: Job, een praktische bijbelverklaring.
  1. Bible. O.T. Job—Commentaries. I. Bible. O.T.
Job—Commentaries. I. Bible. O.T. Job. English.
Revised Standard. 1985. II. Title. III. Series.
BS1415.3.S4513 1985   223'.1077   85-16092

ISBN 0-8028-0101-3

CONTENTS

Translator's Preface	**vii**
Introduction	**1**
The Prologue, 1:1–2:13	**23**
The Great Dialogue, 3:1–31:40	**29**
Job Curses the Day of His Birth, 3:1-26	**29**
First Discourse of Eliphaz, 4:1–5:27	**32**
Job's Answer to the First Discourse of Eliphaz, 6:1–7:21	**37**
Bildad's First Discourse, 8:1-22	**43**
Job's Answer to Bildad's First Discourse, 9:1–10:22	**46**
Zophar's First Discourse, 11:1-20	**53**
Job's Answer to Zophar's First Discourse, 12:1–14:22	**56**
Second Discourse of Eliphaz, 15:1-35	**64**
Job's Reply to the Second Discourse of Eliphaz, 16:1–17:16	**68**
Second Discourse of Bildad, 18:1-21	**73**
Job's Reply to Bildad's Second Discourse, 19:1-29	**75**
Second Discourse of Zophar, 20:1-29	**79**
Job's Reply to Zophar's Second Discourse, 21:1-34	**82**
Third Discourse of Eliphaz, 22:1-30	**86**
Job's Reply to the Third Discourse of Eliphaz, 23:1–24:25	**90**
Bildad's Third Discourse, 25:1-6	**96**
Job's Reply to Bildad's Third Discourse, 26:1-14	**97**
Job's Final Word to his Friends, 27:1-23	**99**
Man Understands All Things, Except the Secret of Life, 28:1-28	**102**
Job Recalls his Former Days of Prosperity and Honor, 29:1-25	**105**
Job Describes his Present State of Misery, 30:1-31	**108**

Job's Great Oath of Innocence, 31:1-40   **112**

Elihu Joins in the Discussion, 32:1-5   **119**

Elihu's First Discourse, 32:6–33:33   **120**

Elihu's Second Discourse, 34:1-37   **126**

Elihu's Third Discourse, 35:1-16   **131**

Elihu's Fourth Discourse, 36:1–37:24   **133**

The First Divine Discourse and Job's Reply, 38:1–39:38   **140**

The Second Divine Discourse and Job's Reply,
    40:1–42:6   **148**

The Epilogue, 42:7-17   **156**

Postscript: The Book of Job and the New Testament   **158**

TRANSLATOR'S PREFACE

In translating this volume from the Dutch original, I have consistently tried to make it both readable and readily useful, for the pastor as well as for the layperson.

Bible quotations are from the Revised Standard Version, except where the author's own translation was closer in letter and spirit to another version. In those cases, I followed the appropriate version—New International, New English, or occasionally other versions—and indicated this in the text. When for some reason the translation was not intelligible without additional explanation, I have supplied a footnote.

It is my earnest wish that users of this commentary may derive as much pleasure and instruction from reading it as I did in translating it.

—JOHN VRIEND

INTRODUCTION

I. THE BOOK

1. Its place in the Old Testament

In the Vulgate—the Latin version of the Bible used predominately in the Roman Catholic Church—as well as in present-day versions of Holy Scripture, Job follows Esther and precedes Psalms. But this is not so in the Hebrew editions of the Old Testament, which divide Scripture into three groups: "the Law" (the first five books of the Bible); "the Prophets" (Joshua, Judges, Samuel, Kings, Isaiah, Jeremiah, Ezekiel, and the twelve "minor" prophets); and "the Writings" (the remaining books recognized as canonical by Judaism and Protestantism). In this last-mentioned group Job comes second, after Psalms and before Proverbs, although some older editions of the Hebrew text place it after Proverbs.

The order in the Vulgate was probably determined by historical considerations: historically, Job was situated in the time of the patriarchs, hence prior to Moses, to whom Psalm 90 was attributed. The Hebrew order, however, probably reflects the order in which the books gained recognition as being sacred. These differences only acquired significance, however, after the books were no longer written down in the form of separate scrolls but were brought together into one volume in our present form, which became standard after the fourth century A.D. At this time it is no longer possible, and hardly meaningful, to introduce changes in the order.

A much more remarkable fact, meanwhile, is that Job was recognized as part of Holy Scripture by both Judaism and Christianity. There are numerous passages in Job's discourses to his friends and to God that neither Jew nor Christian would dare to utter in personal conversation or in prayer. For instance, who among us would dare to say to God, "If I have sinned, what have I done to you, O watcher* of men?" (7:20; NIV). Nevertheless, at the very end of the book (42:7), God reportedly says to Job's friends: ". . . you have not spoken of me what is right, as my servant Job has." What these friends

---

*"Policeman" in author's translation.—Trans.

1

have actually said is much closer to the usual wisdom of our rabbis, priests, and ministers than Job's despairing and—to our minds—all too presumptuous utterances.

It is nothing short of a miracle, therefore, that this book was taken up into the canon of Holy Scripture. We know that, even as late as the first century after Christ, rabbis debated the question of whether books like the Song of Solomon and Ecclesiastes could be regarded as Holy Scripture, but they did not question the inclusion of Job. In addition, the Jewish sect of Qumran, to which we owe the renowned Dead Sea Scrolls, recognized this book as Holy Scripture and even made an Aramaic translation of it. Anyone who has known times of rebellion against God and against the lives he has providentially brought to us can only marvel and gratefully rejoice over the miracle that it is Job—the man who argued with God and men—who is called "my servant," who has spoken right concerning God.

2. *Survey of content*

The book begins with a prose story, embracing chapters 1 and 2, in which we learn about the man Job and hear a conversation between God and "Satan," the prosecuting attorney in the heavenly court. In this dialogue, the Prosecutor states that Job only serves God for the advantage that his piety has brought him, and, in response, God gives him permission to strip Job of all he possesses. Job perseveres in his piety, and the Adversary, in a second conversation with God, gains permission to strike him with a painful illness. Not even Job's wife understands how he can maintain his piety. His three friends visit him but do not know what to say.

From chapter 3 almost to the end of the book, the author writes in poetic form. After seven days Job ends his silence and in his despair curses the day of his birth (3:3-26). The language he uses is so vehement that his friends begin to protest. What follows is a dialogue, in three rounds, between Job and his friends:

4:1–5:27	First discourse of Eliphaz
6:1–7:21	Job's reply
8:1-22	First discourse of Bildad
9:1–10:22	Job's reply
11:1-20	First discourse of Zophar

12:1–14:22 Job's reply
15:1-35 Second discourse of Eliphaz
16:1–17:16 Job's reply
18:1-21 Second discourse of Bildad
19:1-29 Job's reply
20:1-29 Second discourse of Zophar
21:1-34 Job's reply
22:1-30 Third discourse of Eliphaz
23:1–24:25 Job's reply
25:1-6 Third discourse of Bildad
26:1-14 Job's reply

Next, 27:1-23 is Job's answer to the three friends collectively; 28:1-28 is a poem on wisdom, unattainable for man but known to God; 29:1–30:31 is Job's comparison between his earlier prosperity and present suffering; and 31:1-40 is Job's great oath in which he declares himself innocent of a catalogue of sins.

Elihu, a person who has not been mentioned before, is now expressly introduced in 32:1-5. The burden of what he has to say is given is four discourses:

32:6–33:33 First discourse of Elihu
34:1-37 Second discourse of Elihu
35:1-16 Third discourse of Elihu
36:1–37:24 Fourth discourse of Elihu

Job does not reply to the discourses of Elihu.

At last it is God's turn. He addresses himself exclusively to Job: an answer "out of the storm."

38:1–39:33*First discourse of God
39:34-38 Job abstains from replying
40:1–41:25 Second discourse of God
42:1-6 Job recants and repents

In the prose section that follows, God expresses his disapproval of what the three friends have said in their arguments; against them he vindicates Job and restores him to his former state of happiness (42:7-17).

The prose section of chapters 1 and 2 is customarily called the *prologue*, and the concluding section, 42:7-17, the *epilogue*.

---

*From 38:38 to the end of chap. 41, the author is following the versification of the Vulgate.—Trans.

3

3. *The form of the book*

The book of Job is a combination of succinct prose narrative and elaborate poetic dialogues approximating drama. In this regard one could compare it with the late-medieval, so-called Mary-legends of Nijmegen. In our time these have been repeatedly staged before approving audiences, whereas dramatic performances of Job, usually in much abbreviated form, have at most been able to achieve success with a limited public. It is also most unlikely that such use would ever have occurred to the author. Action—which is what the Greek word *drama* means—can really be found only in the prologue and epilogue, hence in the prose narratives, although it must be admitted that their content is very dramatic (1:13-18).

The ancient Near East, whose cultural forms the Old Testament often uses, unlike ancient Greece and ancient India, does not know drama as an art form. From Babylonian literature some dialogues have come down to us (cf. J. B. Pritchard, *Ancient Near Eastern Texts Relating to the Old Testament* [2nd ed., 1955], pp. 437-40) but these, too, lack all action. They are stage dialogues—no more. By comparison, the book of Job comes a little closer to what we call drama, without, however, quite making it. The form is comparatively closer to the Akkadian fable "Dispute between the Date Palm and the Tamarisk" (Pritchard, pp. 410-11), or the Egyptian tale "The Protests of the Eloquent Peasant" (Pritchard, pp. 407-10). In both, after a fairly long narrative introduction, we find discourses and answers, each introduced by narrative statements such as "Then the tamarisk opened its mouth and said . . ." (cf. Job 3:1; 4:1, etc.).

These examples of ancient eastern literature belong to what is usually called Wisdom literature, and to the same category we also assign the book of Job, although as we shall note in section III of this Introduction, it is an emphatic protest against the prevailing wisdom of the time in Israel and the Near East. Should one, after all we have said on the subject, still wish to compare the book of Job with a drama, one will have to refer to the modern theater of the absurd. For the speakers all talk past each other and none of them, with the exception of God, knows what precisely is the issue in Job's trials.

The verse-form in the book follows the ordinary rules of

the ancient Hebrew poem. Generally, every line, coinciding with our present numbered verses, consists of two halves, which often say almost the same thing, frequently complement each other, and sometimes form a contrast. These half-lines [cola] are often, but not always, of the same length. Repeatedly a line consists not of two but of three parts [triad]; this is at times the case when something is affirmed with special emphasis.

Some scholars have attempted to discern a strophic arrangement in the discourses, based on the idea that the same number of lines would each time form a unity of content (strophe). Such an undertaking, however, would force the analyst to deal violently with the text. Over and over he would have to delete, add, or transpose a line. We, on our part, did not feel free to approach the text so surgically. We did, it is true, make divisions in the discourses, not on the basis of a given number of lines but in terms of content. Thus we did arrive at paragraphs—pericopes if you will—of an average of eight lines but often of a greater or lesser number.

4. Place and time of origin

The narrative is set in the southern part of Transjordan, the borderland between Edom and Arabia, a countryside that is half cultivated, half steppe. Eliphaz hails from Teman, a name that elsewhere in the Old Testament designates an Edomitic tribe and landscape. The land of Uz, where Job lived, is also found somewhere in the southeastern part of Transjordan. The author, therefore, situates Job and his friends outside Israelite territory, and although the book is written in Hebrew, one cannot call Job an Israelite. Further, in the discourses the author avoids referring to God by his Israelite name Yahweh, which he does use in chapters 1 and 2, in 42:7-17, where the narrator himself takes the floor, and in the introductions to the divine discourses (38:1; 39:34*; 40:1) and Job's answers to them (39:36*; 42:1). An exception to this occurs in the discourses of Job and his friends in 12:9, which is a quotation from Isaiah 41:20.

The fact that there is extensive reference to the hippopotamus in chapter 40 and to the crocodile in chapter 41 is no reason to suppose that Egypt is the home of the author. In

*See note on p. 3.—Trans.

5

ancient times the tiny Palestinian rivers that issued into the Mediterranean served as habitat for crocodiles (for hippopotami only in much earlier times). Further, the renown of these two animals could have been widespread. In the passage concerning the hippo there is reference also to the Jordan (40:23). So while the locale of the human *dramatis personae* can be determined with some precision there is nothing one can say of the specific environment of the author.

As to the date of the book, what we can determine with certainty is not much more. One reference point is given with the quotation from Isaiah (41:20) in 12:9. Since Isaiah 40–55 is generally dated toward the end of the Babylonian exile, hence shortly before 539 B.C., we will have to date the Book of Job, at least if the Isaiah quotation is not a later addition, after 539. This would be in harmony with the fact that Jesus Sirach, in his litany of praise for the great personalities of Israel's past, alludes to Job immediately after Ezekiel (49:9). We must not, however, credit Sirach with much knowledge of chronology. Furthermore, we have no evidence at all as to how many years or centuries followed the end of the Babylonian exile until the Book of Job originated.

The language of the book shows little kinship with that of the Bible books that are dated in the centuries just before the Christian era. It is a splendid kind of Hebrew: classic in the full sense of the word. Earlier scholarship often ascertained the presence of Aramaic influences on word-forms and meanings, but this is not an argument for a very late date. Even in the days of King Hezekiah, long before the Babylonian exile, the upper classes of Judah were familiar with Aramaic (2 Kings 18:26). In Transjordan the influence of Aram was often paramount (e.g., cf. 2 Kings 10:32-33). In Ezekiel 14:14 and 20, Job is mentioned next to Daniel and Noah as one of the righteous men of an earlier time. But this does not constitute proof that the *Book* of Job already existed then. We do better if we assume an existing oral tradition concerning Job. This tradition cannot be equated with the prose narratives of the prologue and epilogue of the book, however, because, according to Ezekiel 14:19-20, the righteous can save themselves from illness (the plague!), and Job obviously could not. In addition, the epilogue speaks of Job's intercession for his three friends—a prayer that is heard—whereas in Ezekiel 14 the righteous could only save themselves.

One also cannot date the Book of Job on the basis of a presumed development in the spiritual history of Israel. History knows of no such linear, and generally valid, development in concepts and ideas. In every age there are dissidents— and many a Bible book is the product of such dissidents. This is doubtless true of the present book: it continually protests the prevailing opinions of contemporaries, opinions that cannot be dated either, but rather tend to speak for all ages.

The quotation from Isaiah 41:20 recorded in Job 12:9, mentioned earlier, as well as certain resemblances in word usage between Isaiah 40-55 and our book, together constitute an argument for dating the book in the period after the Babylonian exile; the exceptionally fine form of the Hebrew restrains us from coming down to a period after the fifth century B.C. There is no way we can determine the time of origin more precisely.

5. Mode of origination

The idea that the prose story of the prologue and the epilogue first existed independently is not acceptable. Then one would, in any case, have to delete 42:7-9 and 10b, for these verses refer back to what the friends said, and that is recorded in the poetic chapters 4–25. It is, rather, the author's intention to let the prose story serve as a framework around the entire book, as also he introduces each speaker by a prose statement. To this we must add that the prose narrative in the prologue and epilogue, for all its apparent simplicity, displays a number of highly artistic features, which are not at all unworthy of the poet of the chapters 3–31.

It is most probable that the cycle of discourses in 3–31 has not come down to us undamaged. The third round accords to Bildad an abnormally short turn (25:1-6); Job's reply to it (26:1-14) might just as well have been part of a discourse by Bildad or Zophar. And Zophar's third discourse is completely missing. If this is to be attributed to the disappearance of one column from a manuscript, however, then it must have disappeared quite early, for chapters 25 and 26 of the aforementioned Aramaic translation possessed by the Qumran sect reproduces the Hebrew text and this translation dates from around 100 B.C.

It is true that chapter 28 does not fit well between the preceding and succeeding chapters, but it is of such high poetic

7

quality and of such profundity in thought that we do not wish to deny to our poet the authorship of this discourse concerning the elusiveness of wisdom. What we hear in this chapter is not Job so much as the poet, and we may view this song as expressing his conclusions from the discourses—that human wisdom is inadequate in the face of life's riddles, as demonstrated in the failed attempts of the friends to explain Job's lot. The case is different with chapters 34–37, the four discourses of Elihu. If the prologue and the epilogue are part of the original work, then Elihu's discourses cannot have belonged to it, for then there would have been reference to them in the epilogue, just as there is to the discourses of the three friends, whether to declare him wrong along with the three, or to declare him to be right as Job was. Job answers every discourse, as well as those of God, but not those of Elihu. His discourses fall into a pool of overwhelming silence. The contrast between the rather long introduction of Elihu (32:1-6) and the very brief notes of introduction to the discourses of each of the three friends strikes the reader immediately. One could say that this elaborateness is in the nature of an apology. The same digressiveness occurs in the discourses that follow. Elihu's preamble to his first discourse covers no fewer than twenty-two verses (32:6-22; 33:1-7). Whereas we admire the poet of the dialogues between Job and his three friends, among other things, for the richness of his vocabulary, in 33:18-30 Elihu uses one word for "grave" no less than five times, although the repetition has no functional role in the composition.

We may therefore assume that Elihu's discourses do not derive from the poet of Job's history and dialogues; furthermore, on closer scrutiny we see that Elihu's arguments hold no more water than those of his three friends and frequently repeat what they have already said. Presumably, they originated with a later wisdom teacher who felt the book was dangerous literature for inexperienced readers.

On the other hand, we do consider as belonging to the original poetic work the discourses of Yahweh in chapters 38–41, interrupted by Job's replies in 40:1-5 and 42:1-6. Scholars have often viewed the second discourse of Yahweh (40:6–41:34), with its description of the hippo and the crocodile, as a later addition—but for no compelling reason. To the contrary, it was a rule in ancient stylistics to let the most important speaker speak twice. For that matter, there is a discernible difference between, and progression in, the two answers of Job: first, a declaration of impotence (40:4-5), and later one of repentance (42:1-6). The total complex of the divine discourses shows the same literary forcefulness that we have noticed in the dialogues with the friends.

We therefore view the origination of the book as follows: a great poet, in protest against the superficial doctrine of retribution held by his contemporaries, seized upon the figure of Job handed down from remote antiquity as a righteous man; he created around this figure the tale of a wager between the Lord and the Adversary (or Prosecutor, i.e., Satan) as background for Job's sorrowful experiences, putting into the mouths of the friends the doctrine of retribution that prevailed at that time and in that environment, while he expressed his own protest against that stale and shallow doctrine through Job's complaint and indictment. But he went beyond the indictment against an absent God. Over and over Job begs to be allowed to meet God and to hear his voice. Job's God does, at last, appear and speak; the encounter so long desired does take place, and it turns out to be a mind-boggling reality beyond all contradiction.

This same poet later interpolated chapter 28, which is perhaps an existing poem of his own composition that we would be reluctant to have missed even though it does not fit convincingly between the preceding and the following chapters. Later, possibly in a following century, a wisdom teacher inserted chapters 32–37. Perhaps as early as that, parts of the third round of dialogues between Job and his friends had been lost.

The most ancient Greek version of the book, dating from about the beginning of the first century B.C., offers a much shorter text. Perhaps the translator used a manuscript that was damaged at many points; another possibility is that this translator, who had considerably less knowledge of Hebrew than we do, skipped verses he did not understand. The Aramaic translation we have mentioned a number of times, of which we possess roughly 15 percent and that dates from the same period as the Greek version, is based on the same text that we now have in our Hebrew Bibles. The same is true of Jerome's Latin version, the Vulgate, which dates from the fourth century A.D. There is no reason to regard the shorter Greek text as more original than the longer Hebrew text.

II. VIEWS CONCERNING THE BOOK OF JOB

1. *Job is a historical person*

It is altogether understandable that many Bible readers should take the book as the biography of a certain man Job who is assumed to have been a contemporary of the patriarchs. The first words, "There was a man . . . ," are strongly reminiscent of the opening words of 1 Samuel ["There was a certain man . . ."] and Judges 17:1 ["There was a man . . ."]; and there can be no doubt that the authors of these passages intended them as preambles to a piece of history. As we have noted, an ancient story about Job was already in circulation. The names of Job and his three friends are real names, not to be taken as symbolic and certainly not made up by the poet who wrote the book.

Only rarely has Job been identified with the son of Issachar (Gen. 46:13), who is also called Job in many translations, but whose name in Hebrew is spelled differently. In an appendix to the ancient Greek version of the book, Job is identified with Jobab, king of Edom (Gen. 36:33), son of Zerah, who was a grandson of Esau (Gen. 36:10, 13). If this were correct he would have belonged to the fifth generation after Abraham. But the spelling of the names Job and Jobab is too divergent to accept the identification. Historically, we cannot place the person of Job anywhere. We cannot therefore attach any value to the mention of Job's grave in a number of medieval authors; nor to the fact that the well (not a spring!) Enrogel (1 Kings 1:9) has been called "the Well of Job" [Arab. *Bir Ayyub*].

2. *Job is an example*

The view that Job as depicted in the book is meant as an example or model for later believers can, of course, be combined very well with the notion that the book offers a fragment of history, but it is not dependent on it. An early instance of this view may be found in James 5:11: "You have heard of the steadfastness of Job, and you have seen the purpose of the Lord, how the Lord is compassionate and merciful." This statement certainly applies to Job as we get to know him in the prologue and the epilogue, but everything in between witnesses rather to Job's impatience and rebellion. In the preceding verse James says: "As an example of suffering and patience, brethren, take the prophets," but no one is likely to praise the Job of the dialogues and monologues for his resignation in suffering and for his patience.

The exemplaristic view of the book is therefore based solely on the prose story; and we would not advise anyone to follow Job in his vehement addresses to God and his friends. In the discourses of Yahweh (40:2, 8) Job is sharply rebuked, and he accepts these corrections (40:4-5; 42:3), repenting of his overly bold utterances (42:6). We are therefore far from wishing to read the book as entirely exemplary. More precisely, we do not read it at all as an example to be followed in our speech, but we do read it as an example of how a human being suffering physical and spiritual distress may become involved in rebellion against God and man.

3. Job is a parable

This view can already be found in the Talmud where certain rabbis hold forth on it. They probably could not swallow the picture in the prologue in which God enters a wager with the Adversary. It was the less acceptable because our word *Adversary* (or *Prosecutor*) is a translation of the Hebrew word *satan*, which refers to the adversary in a legal trial but which in time became a proper name for the devil (cf. Rev. 12:9-10). So these rabbis saw in Job's history a parable without historical background. No one will maintain that a parable like that of the Good Samaritan is the reproduction of a historical event (even though nowadays "the inn of the Good Samaritan" is pointed out to tourists on the road between Jericho and Jerusalem). But the truth of a story need not be dependent on its place in a historical process.

The characterization of the book of Job as a parable, however, can only have reference to the prologue and not to the epilogue, where the figure of the Adversary is no longer in evidence. One gets the impression that the poet, by not reporting that the Adversary finally had to acknowledge his defeat in the wager, himself indicated that he did not want the reader to view the dialogues between God and the Adversary as historical truth. But we can hardly maintain this characterization of the entire book as a parable, particularly the dialogues between Job, his three friends, and God. The literary genre of the parable, as we know it from the instruction of

Jesus and that of the Talmud, does not tolerate such long expositions.

In conclusion, then, the view that the Book of Job is a parable, though it has some value, fails to explain fully its nature and intent.

4. Job is an allegory

Others have made an attempt to understand the book of Job as an allegory. The suffering of the hero, his unanswered questioning of the reason for his suffering, and his desperate search for a God who does not seem to be willing to give an answer to his complaint and indictment—all this could be an interpretation of the spiritual confusion into which the downfall of state and temple had pitched the Judean people. The distress that came to expression more directly in Lamentations and in many a psalm, especially in Psalm 137 but also in Psalms 44 and 79, for example, also surfaced in the Book of Job, now in the form of an allegory. This view does in fact do justice to the book as a whole, particularly to what Job says to his friends and to God. But if it really were an allegory, then we would have to see Eliphaz, Bildad, and Zophar as portrayals of Job's enemies, not of his friends; that is, of the nations that fought against and trampled on Judah. Thus, one would have to conjure up Assyria, Babylonia, and Edom. But the description of Eliphaz as a Temanite, Bildad as Shuhite, and Zophar as Naamathite excludes such an interpretation. In an allegory all these figures would stand for real entities; but the three friends do not come from different parts of the world, and although they cause Job grief by their attitude and words, they are friends and not hostile powers.

We can imagine that many an oppressed and humiliated people could appropriate Job's complaints for themselves— but such relatively justifiable use of the book does not yet give us the right to make the entire work out to be an allegory.

5. Job has to be understood christologically

In the prologue and epilogue God calls Job "my servant," the same expression we find in the song of the suffering servant of the Lord (Isa. 52:13–53:12). The early Christian church applied this term to Jesus Christ (Acts 4:27). Scripture repeatedly refers to this servant as being righteous and holy. It is true that one could readily imagine Christ quoting certain passages from Job. Anyone wanting to know what Jesus meant when he said to his disciples, "My soul is very sorrowful, even to death . . ." (Mark 14:34), can turn to Job 3; and the many "whys" of Job are echoed in the fourth word from the cross: "My God, my God, why hast thou forsaken me?"

But early Christianity, in pursuance of Isaiah 53 and many words of Christ himself, found the meaning of the suffering of God's holy and righteous servant in the belief that this suffering had atoning and redemptive power: it was "a ransom for many." The idea of vicarious suffering is totally lacking in the Book of Job, however. He himself nowhere speaks, nor do any of his friends, nor does God, of a suffering that would benefit the entire community of humankind. Although we are prepared to admit the relative validity of such a view, at the same time we have to deny that it provides the key to the whole.

III. THE TEACHING OF THE BOOK

The question of how we are to view the book, and what it is teaching us, is not one we can sum up in a sentence. Even if we ignore the parts that interrupt the flow of the book (as pointed out in I.5 of this Introduction) we still have a very complex mass of material left, and one cannot simply unravel it by viewing only what Job says or what God says as the revelational content. Justice has to be done to all parts of the book, and by this rule we can only say that the contradictions between speakers, not only in what Job brings up against the arguments of his friends but also in what Job says when he addresses God, must not in some clever way be resolved into a final harmony. What we have said in the previous section of this Introduction concerning the relative validity of each of the different views of the book also applies to the observations brought forward by the different speakers. We can only proceed step by step and in the end come to the conclusion that we have learned much, not only from Job's discourses but also from the utterances of the other participants in the dialogue. As we proceed one step at a time we observe several points:

1. The book belongs to the category of Wisdom literature

According to *The NIV Complete Concordance* the word *wisdom* occurs in the Book of Job twenty-three times (*Young's Con-*

cordance lists eighteen instances); in addition we find the word *wise*, usually in the nominal form "the wise," seven times. In the Bible the Book of Proverbs is the most characteristic example of this Wisdom literature, but several psalms belong to this category also. Another example is the apocryphal work that we usually designate as Ecclesiasticus, or the Wisdom of Jesus the son of Sirach. However, Wisdom literature is not limited to Israel; there are numerous Sumerian, Babylonian, and Egyptian collections that also have to be included in this category. Wisdom literature is international; that is the reason why the specifically Israelite name "Yahweh" occurs only rarely in the biblical Wisdom books, a rule that applies also to chapters 3–37 of the present book. The wise men of Edom were very famous (Obad. 8-9; cf. Jer. 49:7); it comes as no surprise, therefore, that our author situates the history of Job in the borderland between Edom and Arabia.

This wisdom is the precipitate of human insight but not, for that reason, areligious. The wise man is one who reckons seriously with the divine government of this world; and often in the Bible "folly" is a synonym for "sin." Jeremiah (18:18) mentions the wise man, the priest, and the prophet as three distinct but related figures in the life of the people. The wise man is he who possesses true insight into the course of human life and who—equally important!—lets himself be governed in all his actions by this insight. Without its application to life wisdom is useless knowledge.

One can only have the greatest respect for this wisdom. It introduces order into the chaotic conditions of life and excludes the arbitrary, also the arbitrariness of fate and the rule of the accidental. It teaches human beings that they are responsible for the consequences of their deeds. It becomes so basic and so general that God's dealings with humanity also are placed under its propitious rule; in fact, wisdom is called the first of God's creatures (cf. Prov. 8:22-31).

2. *The book protests the prevailing wisdom*

In the notion that wisdom is the guiding principle also of God's actions, there may lurk a great danger. This is not so if one lets God's wisdom be God's; but it is dangerous if one equates it with human insight. Then the assumption is that a person can trace God's reasonings, even predicting how he will react to human deeds. One then detracts from God's sovereign freedom. Then, moreover, the reality in which we live will often prove to be at odds with our expectations. Rather than being a warning against thoughtless actions, wisdom is made into a system that people even impose upon God's freedom; and if the realities of our lives do not comport with the system, well then, it is too bad for the facts! System then overrules reality and people act as if their "wisdom" can solve all of life's riddles.

But life cannot be forced into the Procrustean bed of system. What the Dutch poet de Génestet wrote is still true: "It is as though this riddling present life / In sadness ridicules each clever scheme." Any person with a strong sense of reality discovers sooner or later that every theory concerning life encounters elements that do not fit under general headings.

Such realism is what the authors of Scripture display. Two books in the Old Testament constitute protests against the hypertrophy of wisdom as it apparently manifested itself in some wisdom teachers of the time. They are Ecclesiastes and Job, both of which must be classified as Wisdom literature but which dissent strongly from the prevailing views of wisdom. In this regard Ecclesiastes proceeds more from personal observation of human society, although personal experience occasionally comes to expression in the form of play or experiment. Job, on the other hand—and we shall now roughly equate him with the poet who wrote the book—speaks out of the bitterness of his soul, putting into words his disappointment, suffering, doubts, and desperation. In a nutshell, then, Ecclesiastes is an intellectual game, Job an existential cry.

According to the wisdom that prevailed in the social environment in which these books were written, misfortune always follows in the wake of moral evil. It has to. Ecclesiastes observes that this rule does not always apply in the world; Job experiences the inadequacy of it in his own experience. It is primarily at this point that both books lodge their protest. But in Job the protest is more impassioned, the reason being that his friends do not only witness to the blessedness of the godly and the misfortune that attends evildoers but infer from the misfortune that strikes a person that he is guilty. Job just has to take this personally, for his friends have come to talk with him about his misfortune—to "comfort" him. But it would have been dishonest and hypocritical for Job to have followed the advice of his friends and to have accepted his suffering as just punishment for his sins. What the friends assert may be true in general but Job is not interested in generalities—his concern is his own personal misery.

3. *The book operates on different levels*

We now face what is both the biggest difficulty of the book and the best key to understanding it. Over against the rather simple life-and-world view implicit in the prevailing wisdom as represented by the three friends, the author posits reality in all its complexity—including extramundane reality. There is not just an issue between Job and his three friends, there is also an issue between God and the Adversary—an existential one, at that. There is a discussion in the heavenly court about Job; decisions are made concerning him that are carried out and affect him in flesh and marrow.

Not much in Job's complaints refers directly to the prologue, but there is no doubt that in reading the book one must continually bear the prologue in mind. Job is involved in a struggle with his friends but, without his or their knowing it, God is also involved in a dispute with the Adversary. If Job were to lose his battle, God would lose his. In the celestial dispute it is Job's performance that is at stake. At stake, too, is God's honor, that is, his existence as God. God wants to see vindicated his confidence in his servant Job. To that extent the book is a kind of *theodicy*, a justification of God: God must be vindicated against the Adversary. But at the same time, and in no less a measure, the book is an *anthropodicy*, a justification of man: a justification of this one man Job. To generalize, then, God's vindication consists in the fact that there really are people on earth who do not serve God for the sake of any material or spiritual advantage but for his sake.

It is noteworthy, in this connection, that whereas the three friends in their discourses exclusively address Job, Job himself, at least in the first round and in his reply to Eliphaz's second discourse, repeatedly moves from a reply to these people to a complaint to God. Further on, this direct address to God ends, but it comes back in Job's final long discourse (30:20-23). This is an indication that the focus of the book is not just philosophical discussion but the fact that God is directly and personally involved in Job's soul-searching. Thus, throughout the book the issue is simultaneously God's honor *and* Job's.

The dialogues, too, serve as medium for this multilevel concern of the author. It is far from being the case that one simply has to reject what the friends say as untrue. The author has not turned them into caricatures. He accepts the relative validity of their arguments. That is why a statement of Eliphaz (Job 5:13) is cited in 1 Corinthians 3:19 as an authoritative pronouncement of Scripture. The situation with the positions of the three friends is that in general one has to agree with their arguments but deny—as Job does—that these general truths are applicable to Job's case.

The same thing can also be said of Elihu's four speeches. We have stated earlier (I.5) that these cannot have been written by the poet who wrote the book as a whole. That is not to say that they are worthless, however. Rather, they contain a large number of good ideas worthy of being laid to heart. To be sure, most of what Elihu brings up has already been said by the three friends; still, we would be reluctant to have to forgo a passage like 33:23-30. Although our estimate of this work, composed by a later wisdom teacher, is not as high as that of the poetry of the writer of the whole, it is still remarkable that 32:18-19 inspired the Dutch poet Joost van den Vondel to compose these lines in his *Roskam*:

. . . But that which lay at my heart's bottom
Is spurting upward to the throat; I am bottled up
Like yeasty wine that's bursting to the bung.

Elihu intends to take a position in between the friends and Job (32:2-3), and although he does not quite succeed, his discourse still occurs at a somewhat different level from the argumentations of Eliphaz, Bildad, and Zophar. In this manner this large interpolation, inserted later, makes its own contribution to the total impression that the book makes on us at several levels.

On the whole, the book remains for us above all a testimony that the human condition is full to bursting of insoluble riddles. It denies that the wisdom that the friends represent has the answer. There is much in human life that can be explained neither as reward for irreproachable conduct nor as punishment for sins committed. This riddle is all the more painful because the book, in distinction from Psalms 49 and

73, for instance, opens no windows on a life after death (not even in 19:25-27, at least if we have caught the meaning in our translation and commentary). Job demands that he be vindicated and saved in this earthly life. He insists that God will maintain his right(s) here and now.

For that reason he often expresses the wish that this God, whom he does not see anywhere•nor ever hear, will at last appear personally, so that the sufferer can plead his cause before his judgment seat (13:13-28; 19:23-27; 23:3-7; 31:35-37). From the God who has afflicted him he appeals to the God who is his advocate (16:19-21) and bondsman for the righteous.

The wish comes true in the discourses of Yahweh (chaps. 38–41). But does this solve the problem of the righteous sufferer? In no way. In essence God adds nothing that was not said by our poet in chapter 28: human wisdom is inadequate to explain the riddles of life and the mystery of divine government. Creation as a whole is full of riddles for man, who is accustomed to let all things turn on himself as pivot. Of what use is the wild donkey or the buffalo to the farmer? What use to people are the hippos and the crocodiles? God gives no answers to Job: he poses questions to him.

Job answers God but not his questions. He declares himself powerless (39:36-37) and admits that he has spoken hastily without understanding (42:1-4). Now he has seen God, as he had wished, although it does not say in so many words that God had not only spoken out of the storm but had shown himself to Job. But there is no need: the point is not that Job wanted to see God with the sense of sight; it is that he wanted to meet God in a personal encounter. In this encounter he lost all desire to say the things he had planned to ask before the judgment seat of God: "Therefore I recant and repent in dust and ashes" (42:6).

This is hardly a solution and it is no wonder that we remain unsatisfied. But that is *our* problem. We have probably only read the divine discourses and have to acknowledge along with Job: "My ears had heard of you." One must not just read these awesome chapters, however, but undergo them. Then there is a chance that we shall be led to say with Job, ". . . but now my eyes have seen you" (42:5b). A Reality beyond reason is revealed to us and we are delivered from our preoccupation with ourselves and our fate. We are no longer bent over ourselves in total absorption but now cast ourselves down before God's sovereign freedom, the sovereignty of him who makes himself known and is equally near to all. In such surrender there is an ecstasy in which all questions are silenced. "In that day you will no longer ask me anything" (John 16:23).

We have almost forgotten the epilogue. After the ecstasy experienced in self-humiliation, follows the resurrection of the body: Job regains all that he had lost. So the end returns to the beginning, for without knowing it, Job has won God's dispute with the Adversary: he has proven, even in agony and despair, that a person can serve God without seeking his own advantage. In extreme anguish, abandoned by his wife and friends, he clung to God even when it seemed that God had turned against him. Not another word is said about the Adversary: Job has put him to shame and he has taken a hasty leave. If after this one still wanted to summarize the complex teaching of the book, we could say the following:

1. In one's struggles and suffering as a human being one can, without knowing it, struggle and suffer for God's honor.
2. An important part of this struggle and suffering is to question the course of this world and to despair over one's own lot.
3. Human wisdom has some validity with regard to all this, but leaves many riddles unsolved.
4. One may not gratuitously apply the general rules of human wisdom to every special case.
5. If in struggle and pain one comes to a personal encounter with God, all one's questions melt away.

IV. OUR METHOD IN TRANSLATION AND ELUCIDATION; THE AIDS USED

1. Our method in translation

As much as possible we have held to the text as it is found in the printed editions of the Hebrew Bible. We only very rarely ventured to emend the text. The more we delve into the Hebrew Bible—with the aid of enormously expanded knowledge of both the cognate languages and the ancient eastern way of life—the more we are convinced that the text of many Bible books, also that of Job, deserves much more confidence than earlier generations of Bible scholars tended to repose in them.

In those days texts were often emended on the basis of what research into the ancient Greek and other translations of antiquity produced in the way of illumination. We have seen, however, that the Greek translator offers a much shorter text, one that cannot be regarded as more original than the Hebrew, and that he often understood little of the Hebrew. In other ancient translations as well, there is considerable evidence that our predecessors misunderstood the Hebrew. For that reason, having access to the somewhat improved knowledge of the Hebrew presently at our disposal, we have stuck with the text handed down to us by the Jews, and declined to take the liberty of deleting a verse or passage here and there.* We did come to the conclusion that the discourses of Elihu do not belong to the work of our poet (see under I.5), but we also asserted (III.3) that these chapters still have their value. Therefore, with a signal to the reader, we have let them stand at the place they actually occupy.

There is not another book with so many words that occur only once in the entire Hebrew Bible. This fact presents great difficulties to the translator, which he can only try to solve with the help of languages related to the Hebrew. Even in instances where words occur that one also finds in other parts of Hebrew Scripture, we sometimes question whether the poet uses these words in another sense or with another nuance than have other writers.

So the translator often has to make a choice between various possibilities. This introduces a subjective element in his work. He will, of course, consult the studies produced by fellow scholars in the field and, in instances where proposed renderings do not satisfy him, fall back on his own insight and knowledge. In a commentary like the present one, which is not intended for philologists, there is no room for argumentation that operates with Ugaritic, Babylonian, Aramaic, or Arabic materials. It is the purpose of the author to treat, in professional journals, a number of instances in which he champions a different view from the one held until now; but until that is done the reader will simply have to trust that deviations, not in wording but in understanding, from the established Bible translations are the result of fresh and seri-

*But see note on p. 3.—Trans.

ous scholarship. The meaning of the whole will not be affected by these proposals.

2. Our method in elucidation

To enhance the readability of the commentary we have, as regards the dialogues, followed a different method than has, to our knowledge, ever been employed before in commentaries on Job. In the commentary proper we have let the different speakers speak for themselves. This approach is in harmony with the "staged dialogue" character of almost the entire book—but would obviously not be applicable to other books of the Bible.

This peculiarity in method will create no difficulties for one who reads the commentary in its entirety from beginning to end—which is what we hope for. The case is different when a reader simply wants to check out a certain text or passage. He could possibly mistake the identity of a speaker and ascribe a given passage to one of the three friends when in actual fact the speaker is Job. To avoid this confusion we have inserted an introductory statement before every discourse and noted the name of the speaker at the beginning of every section. It is our hope that this will prevent the possible confusion we have referred to.

3. The aids used

In the course of centuries an enormous amount of literature has accumulated around the Book of Job.* J. H. Kroeze, in his commentary, offers a list of more than three hundred commentaries and studies. Most of these assume that the reader knows Hebrew. The present writer naturally could not take note of all this material. Much of the older literature had been assimilated in J. C. Matthes, *Het boek Job* (2 vol., 1865). Nearly a century later the work of J. H. Kroeze, just referred to, appeared: *Het boek Job verklaard* (Commentaar op het Oude Testament, 1961), where many of the newer insights are subjected to acute and critical evaluation. In addition I used a number of non-Dutch commentaries; among others, that of R. Gordis, *The Book of Job* (Moreshet Series, Studies in Jewish History. Literature and Thought II, 1978).

These were aids to the author; they are not necessarily

*See next section for suggested commentaries in English.—Trans.

21

available to the readers of this commentary. With them no knowledge of Hebrew is assumed.

V. LITERATURE

Andersen, F. I. *Job: An Introduction and Commentary.* Tyndale Old Testament Commentaries. Edited by D. J. Wiseman. London/Downers Grove, Inter-Varsity Press, 1976.

Barth, K. *Church Dogmatics.* IV/3. Translated by G. W. Bromiley. Edited by G. W. Bromiley and T. F. Torrance. Edinburgh: T. & T. Clark, 1961. Pp. 383-461.

Davidson, A. B. *The Book of Job.* The Cambridge Bible for Schools and Colleges. Cambridge: Cambridge University Press, 1884.

Delitzsch, F. *Job.* Translated by F. Bolton. Reprint. Grand Rapids: Wm. B. Eerdmans Publishing Co., n.d.

Dhorme, E. *A Commentary on the Book of Job.* Translated by H. Knight. 1967. Reprint. Nashville: Thomas Nelson Publishers, 1984.

Driver, S. R. and G. B. Gray. *A Critical and Exegetical Commentary on the Book of Job.* The International Critical Commentary. 1921. Reprint. Edinburgh: T. & T. Clark, 1977.

Glatzer, N. H. *The Dimensions of Job: A Study and Selected Readings.* New York: Schocken Books, 1969.

Gordis, R. *The Book of God and Man: A Study of Job.* 1965. Reprint. Chicago/London: The University of Chicago Press, 1978.

_____. *The Book of Job: Commentary, New Translation, and Special Studies.* New York: KTAV, 1977.

Habel, N. C. *Job.* Knox Preaching Guides. Edited by J. H. Hayes. Atlanta: John Knox Press, 1981.

_____. *The Book of Job.* The Cambridge Bible Commentary on the New English Bible. Cambridge: Cambridge University Press, 1975.

Hartley, J. E. *The Book of Job.* The New International Commentary on the Old Testament. Edited by R. K. Harrison. Grand Rapids: Wm. B. Eerdmans Publishing Co., forthcoming.

Murphy, R. E. *The Psalms, Job.* Proclamation Commentaries. 1977. Reprint. Philadelphia: Fortress Press, 1982.

Rowley, H. H. *Job.* The New Century Bible Commentary. Edited by R. E. Clements and M. Black. Rev. ed. London: Marshall, Morgan & Scott, 1976. Reprint. Grand Rapids: Wm. B. Eerdmans Publishing Co., 1980.

Terrien, S. T. *Job: Poet of Existence.* Indianapolis: The Bobbs-Merrill Company, 1957.

Vischer, W. "God's Truth and Man's Lie: A Study of the Message of the Book of Job." Translated by D. G. Miller. *Interpretation* 11 (1961): 131-46.

Westermann, C. *The Structure of the Book of Job: A Form-Critical Analysis.* Translated by C. A. Muenchow. Philadelphia: Fortress Press, 1981.

THE PROLOGUE 1:1–2:13

JOB'S PIETY

Long ago, in the land of the tribe of Uz (cf. Jer. 25:20; Lam. 4:21), where the highlands of Edom merge into the Arabian desert, there lived a very special man. His father, who is not known to us, gave him the name Job; its meaning is uncertain. Inwardly and outwardly decent, he treated his fellowman with all fairness; he had the profoundest respect for God and thorough aversion to all evil. His wife, whose voice comes through briefly in 2:9, gave him seven sons and three daughters; he was more than happy. His enormous herds of sheep and camels grazed in the Arabian grassland; his oxen served to pull the plow on his extensive landholdings more to the northwest, where also his donkeys were used for the transportation of products and equipment. To run such a mixed enterprise of cattle raising and agriculture he had—as was the custom in the economy of those days—numerous slaves. He was known as the wealthiest of all the inhabitants of the East, the border country where Transjordan slowly passes into the Arabian desert.

His sons were already independent, presumably married, and lived in their own homes. These homes were so situated that from their locations each one could oversee and manage a part of the family estate. In view of its size they must have lived at some considerable distance from each other and from Job, but they did uphold family ties. On festive occasions, such as the time of sheep shearing in the spring or the conclusion of the vintage in the fall, the brothers came together at banquets, the first day at the home of the oldest, the second day at the home of the second oldest, and so on, for a whole week. Their sisters, who had never left home, were also invited.

After the week of feasting had run its course they all came to the parental home. There a day was spent in bathing and washing in preparation for the solemn sacrifice of the next day. Early the next morning, like the ancient patriarchs, Job would then act as priest for his entire family and offer a burnt offering in expiation for possible violations of the standards of piety committed under the influence of wine at the feast of the previous week; for every child a sheep or a goat was put on the altar to compensate for possible shortcomings in the children's lives. It could be that prosperity had gone to the heads of the celebrants and made them think, "Now I do not need God anymore. The storehouses are full. For the rest of the year we can take care of ourselves. Farewell God—see you next year!" Job loved his children and had the deepest respect for God; so by his sacrifices he made everything right again between those two.

1:6-12 THE ADVERSARY CHALLENGES THE LORD

From that idyllic setting on earth the story now moves to the court of heaven. This is pictured in earthly terms—not to be taken literally, of course—as a royal court where the Lord, the God of Israel, grants audiences to his servants, here called "the sons of God," that is, inhabitants of heaven. Among the royal officials there is also the "Satan," a Hebrew name that means "Adversary," like the Greek name "diabolos" from which our word "devil" is derived. In ancient times a king was first of all a judge; to his court belonged an "adversary" who like a prosecuting attorney in our courts fulfilled an essential function in the practice of law. So, in our story, the Adversary is not an opponent of God, however cynical and insolent he may be, but in his way he upholds God's honor by reporting the shortcomings of people. For that purpose he crisscrosses the whole earth in every direction, with eyes and ears wide open to report whatever evil he has observed.

Whenever people try to depict divine matters in human imagery, they always bog down somewhere. So it goes here. It turns out that God does not really need an Inspector-General like the Adversary: God himself knows perfectly well who serves him and who does not. So he is thoroughly familiar with that excellent man, Job, who is not only the wealthiest man in the East but morally and religiously without equal on earth.

In the opinion of the Adversary, Job's piety, and therefore all human piety, is a refined form of egoism: by being pious a person gains for himself security and prosperity, for God protects the pious together with their possessions. If a person derived no gain from proper behavior, he would act very differently. To prove this, the Adversary challenges the Lord to adopt a different policy for once and to withhold protection from Job. Then what will happen? The Adversary swears that all that pious talk and conduct would be a thing of the past. Robbed of his wealth Job will bid God farewell: "I no longer need you; you do not even want to protect me anymore." That which Job feared his children might think only in their hearts at some unguarded moment, he himself will then throw openly, and in full awareness of what he is saying, into God's face.

God accepts the challenge; he has no doubts about his servant Job. Job does not serve God for something he can gain by it, but because he is the Lord God. And because the Lord not only trusts Job but also loves him, he puts the Adversary under one limitation: he must not touch Job's person; that is, he must spare his life and health.

1:13-22 JOB LOSES EVERYTHING

It was again the season of feasting, and on the first day all of Job's children were guests in the home of the oldest son. As was his custom Job himself had stayed at his own home.

A messenger comes running and pictures the situation on and around the field where the oxen were plowing—which suggests that it was in the time of the autumn feast—and describes how men and animals were attacked by Sabeans, a tribe that formerly lived in northwest Arabia, later in southern Arabia. Attacking and carrying off other people's cattle always was a favorite sport among Arabs but, as a rule, not so many lives were lost as was the case here. The slaves paid for their loyalty to their good masters with their lives.

The second message of misfortune concerns Job's small stock. All bunched together, as animals will do in extremely bad weather, they were struck, together with the shepherds on duty, by a bolt of lightning.

The third messenger announces the loss of Job's camels. The Chaldeans were originally a group of Aramean tribes, of which some settled in Syria and some down the Euphrates river valley. Apparently there were also some bands that lived in the desert and undertook raids from there. An attack from three sides is the best way to drive the stock in the direction desired by the attackers. There is considerable resemblance between the third report and the first.

The fourth messenger, like the second, reports a natural disaster: a whirlwind swept in and overturned the house of the oldest son so that he, together with his brothers and sisters, was buried in the ruins. This fourth disaster is self-evidently the worst of all; as a result of it Job lost everything that gave meaning to his wealth. What he has left—his wife, four slaves, and his own house—means little to him without his children.

In time of mourning it is not fitting to wear fine clothing; mourners tear their clothes. Similarly, they shave off locks of hair, which were otherwise the ornaments of the head. After satisfying the demands of the conventions of the day, Job demonstrates his respectful submission to the unfathomable will of God by throwing himself on his knees, extending his torso forward until, supporting himself on his hands, he touches the ground with his forehead. This is how one honored kings and gods.

In four lines of verse Job summarizes his life from the cradle to the grave. He clearly expects nothing more from his life. Just as he came naked—that is, without any possessions of his own—into the world, so he will go down to his grave poor and destitute. The mother's womb and the womb of the earth are equated more often in poetry (cf. Ps. 139:13-15). Job's wealth, of which such proud mention was made in 1:2-4, had not been brought with him at birth, but was only a temporary, gratuitous gift from the hand of God. Job finds no reason for making accusations to God; on the contrary, he has to be thankful to God for the blessings he has enjoyed for so many years. God is fully within his rights in taking back from Job the possessions he has given to him on loan. It is only proper to thank God afterward for his interest-free loans: "blessed be the name of the Lord" means we shall, together with the whole creation, mention his name in grateful obedience.

With regard to Job's conduct, following a train of disasters, it needs to be said that he made no misstep in any way whatsoever; not an improper word crossed his lips. The Adversary expected that Job would take his leave from God— send God packing, so to speak—but God's confidence in Job is not put to shame: Job's piety is no mask for self-interest.

2:1-7a THE ADVERSARY AGAIN CHALLENGES
THE LORD

A second assembly of God's heavenly entourage is described in the same words as the first (1:6-8). The question addressed by the King to the Adversary, "Where have you come from?" is worded [in Hebrew] a touch differently than in 1:7, to indicate perhaps that the Lord knows that the Adversary has lost his case and expects him to acknowledge it. But the Adversary gives precisely the same answer as the first time, and the Lord again has to steer the dialogue in the direction of Job. What was said of Job in chapter one, both by the author and by God, is still in force: morally and religiously Job is without an equal among his contemporaries. Even after Job has been stripped of everything he had, without having deserved his misfortune by having committed some gross sin, he remains a man of unimpeachable integrity.

The Adversary answers with a proverb that literally reads "skin for skin"; that is, a person who is in difficulties, whatever they are, will if necessary give up all his possessions provided he himself comes out unscathed. Job has lost much, but not his health. His whole bearing will change if he is brought to the edge of death by illness!

God accepts the new challenge—a sign of his unlimited trust in Job. But he does not want to lose his faithful servant; thus the Adversary is allowed to make Job deathly ill, but he may not let him die.

2:7b-10 JOB GETS SICK

All of a sudden Job's entire body breaks out in painful blotches and sores. It is not leprosy, therefore; that disease comes only very gradually. We cannot say exactly what it is, nor must we try to discover it by inference from Job's complaints in the following chapters where the poet describes human suffering of various kinds. This much is sure: Job has to endure intense pain and an unbearable itch. Since the days of mourning over the death of his children began, he no longer sat on a chair or a bench but on the ground in front of his house—in the sand.

It is all too much for his wife. To have to watch someone

suffer without being able to help can fill a person with un-reasonable resentment toward the patient. That is what happens to her; she longs for the end and the shortest route to it runs through a conflict with God. Without knowing it she is working to help the Adversary: "Send God packing, then you will be dead soon!"

Job's response, under the circumstances, is still gentle: it seems she thinks and talks like a hussy off the street, although all these years she has been his faithful marriage partner. If she will stop to think she will see that whoever accepts God's blessings has no choice but to accept also his trials. The conclusion of this episode is the same as the one following the story of Job's first trials: he remains unblameable in his conduct. Even now no improper word has crossed his lips.

2:11-13 A SICK-VISIT FROM THREE FRIENDS

Job's friends probably came from the same country, Edom, that Job did himself. Eliphaz occurs as an Edomite name in Genesis 36:4, 10, and 15, and Teman is a district, perhaps also a city, somewhere in Edom. Bildad is a descendant of Shuah, a son of Abraham and Keturah, sent away by his father to the land of the East (Gen. 25:1-6). Like Job, Bildad was an "Easterner." About Zophar, his descent and place of residence, we do not know anything.

After meeting to consult each other the three friends join to look up Job to express their sympathy and possibly to point out to him the positive elements in his suffering. From a distance they do not even recognize him, disfigured as his face is by sores. In ancient times adult men were not ashamed to show sorrow or sympathy by weeping loudly. Job's mourning becomes their own—something they signal by tearing their own outer clothing. This action, and also the act of throwing dust on their heads, by which they made themselves look like the buried dead, is proof that they had first of all come to grieve with Job over the death of his children. For that reason they also sit, like Job, on the bare ground. But the hideous appearance presented by Job's running sores was for them an unexpected horror, which silenced all the words of consolation they intended to speak. Words are helpless against pain. As people who enter into Job's life and feelings, they share silently in Job's misery.

THE GREAT DIALOGUE 3:1–31:40

JOB CURSES THE DAY OF HIS BIRTH 3:1-26

We are still informed in prose that at the end of seven days of silence the sufferer finally breaks the silence—as Jeremiah did at a deep point of despair (Jer. 20:14-18)—to pronounce a curse upon the day of his birth. In ancient times people thought that by cursing someone they could break the relationship between him and his god; figuratively, to curse the day of one's birth means, therefore, that this day no longer belongs to the cycle of the year as God has ordained and regulated it. That comes to expression here and there in Job's curse, but more prominent in it is Job's despair of the meaning of his existence. Job is not now addressing his friends, nor God; he only gives expression to his own chaotic state of feeling and being, without thinking of any listeners.

His lament is divided in three parts of nearly equal length:

3:3-10	If only I had never been born!
3:11-19	If only I had died at birth!
3:20-26	What meaning does an existence like mine have?

3:3-10 IF ONLY I HAD NEVER BEEN BORN!

Day and night together form a twenty-four-hour period and it is this period which I, Job, now curse. Whether I saw the light of life during the day or at night, people said of my mother: "It is a male person she has carried in her womb"— among us this is a greater reason for joy than the birth of a daughter. That twenty-four-hour period must pass from the scene—no longer make its appearance in the yearly succession of days. Let darkness take the place of that day and let God, who regulates the times, not inquire into it. Let no light-signal announce its turn to put in its appearance. Let it be established by law that this twenty-four-hour period, now and in perpetuity, belongs to the darkness as its rightful territory, and let an impenetrable cloud set itself over it as its keeper. Should that day still risk making an appearance, then let the new owner, the darkness, come to block the light of the sun, be it by an eclipse or a duststorm, to frustrate all resistance. Let the darkness, in which no forms or figures can be recognized, take that period away as plunder so that it can never again take its place in the cycle of the year. In that night let no child ever be born; let no shout of joy, such as was heard at my birth, ever penetrate that darkness.

Should my curse not be strong enough, let the imprecations of the professionals be added, the magicians who can turn that part of the calendar into a day of misfortune and create confusion in a well-ordered cosmos with its celestial bodies, and provoke the ancient chaos monster, Leviathan, who was defeated by the Creator, into renewed action. Do not ask me if I regard as true the claims of these practitioners of black magic. That is not a question a person in my situation even raises. I do not even know if my own imprecations do anything, but curse I will.

Let that day be total darkness, from its first beginnings (Gen. 1:5ff.) when in the evening twilight the first stars begin to shine, to the dawn that otherwise appears, as well as the following twelve hours of daylight. Like the watchmen of Psalm 130:6, let that day look for the first glimmerings of light, the eyelids of the dawn, but in vain; the entire twenty-four-hour period must remain pitch-dark. All this I want because in that period the womb of my mother opened to bring me as a baby into the world. If that had not happened, then I would not have experienced all this misery. Unlike the prophet Jeremiah (15:10) I will not charge my mother with any wrongdoing; my anger concerns that day alone and, really, I only want to say: I wish I had never been born.

3:11-19 IF ONLY I HAD DIED AT BIRTH!

If only I had been one of those innumerable children who come into the world dead or dying. Considering the grief I now experience the care spent on me as an infant was a disservice done me. The midwife, sitting on her knees, caught me when I was born and after bathing me gave me to my mother to be nursed. Were those acts of love, acts of respect for the newborn life? It may be, but neglect, followed by a speedy death, would have been better for me. Then I would not have suffered all this grief over the loss of my children and possessions and all this pain from my illness. I would then immediately have passed to the abode of the dead—the everlasting sleep—which will also be the portion of the mightiest people on this earth, when after a lifetime of building and fortifying their cities they will be carried away by death.

O, to have died at birth—or even without ever having lived, to have been buried under ground without any ceremony like a stillborn child—that, compared with my present existence, seems to me an enviable lot (Eccles. 6:3-5). In the realm of death there is rest. The scoundrels, whose only goal in life it was to increase their power and wealth with whatever means they could, lie just as quietly there as the poor devils they exploited, the victims whose life expired from hard labor. There the slaves who worked long hours under the supervision of brutal overseers at last find peace. They no longer hear the bark of the slavedriver's voice. In death there is neither class nor rank. Whether a person is small, poor, of lowly origins and little status, or big, someone who does not have to lick anyone's boots, in death they are all alike. There a slave becomes a freeman: his former master has no say in the realm of the dead. Certainly, I was big—in possessions, in prosperity, in good fortune and happiness—but all of that has for me become meaningless in my present state. If only I had died at birth!

3:20-26 WHAT MEANING DOES AN EXISTENCE LIKE MINE HAVE?

Just what does a wretched man, one who can no longer handle life, get out of his existence? Just why is the light of life given— I will not even mention God—to someone who will soon have to drink the bitter cup to the dregs? What sense is there in continuing a life that no longer arouses any expectations for the future and can only make one long for the end? If only the end would come! Like someone who knows the place where a treasure is hidden and digs for it with joy and eagerness, so, and even more eagerly, do I long to meet my death. It would be a joy for me to discern with my mind's eye the grave intended for me together with the stone that will be rolled in front of it. My way is no longer clear to me; I can see no way to do anything meaningful. God—if I may still refer to him for a moment—has barricaded my way forward and on both sides with thornbushes, so that there is no longer any escape for me.

Just as people begin and end the day with food, so every day begins and ends for me with sighing and grief. I continually groan with pain, a sound like the distant drone of a waterfall. All that a person can rightly fear has come over me.

In my physical and spiritual distress I cannot find peace or rest anywhere. I am in a state of utter perplexity and collapse. I no longer understand a thing about human life and there is no answer to my "Why?" Just what meaning does an existence like mine still have?

FIRST DISCOURSE OF ELIPHAZ 4:1–5:27

Eliphaz, who heads the list of the three friends (2:11), is also the first in whose mouth the author puts a discourse. The poet does not turn the friends into caricatures; much of what they say is true for all times. For that reason Paul, in 1 Corinthians 3:19, can cite a verse from Eliphaz's discourse (5:13) as an authoritative word of Scripture. Much of what Eliphaz presents in these two chapters is fully worthy of our reflection.

The first course of Eliphaz can be divided into six parts:

4:2-6	Now accept a lesson for your own life!
4:7-11	Every human being gets what he asks for.
4:12-21	This was confirmed to me by a vision.
5:1-7	Misfortune is the fruit of wrongdoing.
5:8-16	God can reverse misfortune.
5:17-27	Then all will be well again.

4:2-6 NOW ACCEPT A LESSON FOR YOUR OWN LIFE!

Would you, Job, in your profound distress, be able to tolerate a word from someone else? I, Eliphaz, can no longer remain silent: my heart is very full and after what you have said I can no longer restrain myself. In former days it was you who spoke words of encouragement to people who had gotten into difficulties; you pointed out the right way for them to go in all kinds of problems, and by your words people without hope were given new strength. When someone was about to stumble in a moral sense, your admonition kept him from falling; when someone's knees were shaking from fear, then with a firm statement of guidance you knew how to restore his courage.

But now a heavy ordeal has come upon you and one might expect that you would speak to yourself the same strong words with which you used to address others. "Physician, heal yourself!" (Luke 4:23). But we see the opposite happen: now you yourself are breaking under the strain of your suffering. Now that misfortune has struck you and not others, you sit down in utter disarray and know no way out. As a God-fearing man in word and deed, you were always full of self-confidence. Your integrity, of which you were very sure, made you expect the best of things. Well, it turned out differently. So now apply the words you used to speak to others in their suffering to your own situation. Now accept a lesson for your own life!

4:7-11 EVERY HUMAN BEING GETS WHAT HE ASKS FOR

It is true: you are now severely ill and you suffer unbearable pain, but where there is life, there is hope. A blameless man of integrity is not simply taken away in the bloom of life. The case is different with the ungodly: they soon perish. They are the people who take advantage of others; they plunge their fellow human beings into disaster and poverty—for example, by mercilessly demanding payment of outstanding debts. When people are unable to pay them, the creditor takes their pitiful little field away from them or forces them into slavery (2 Kings 4:1). A person who inflicts such misery on others will soon come to grief himself. God is a God of strict justice; he only needs to blow a bit, and *phtt*! gone is the cruel man of wealth. God's anger knows exactly how to find him, for his wrath is just—irresistible as the stormwind.

Riches and power go hand in hand. I want to compare the unbridled capitalist with the most dangerous predator— the lion. One is frightened just listening to the roars and growls of the lion family; that is, to the boasting of these men of wealth and their families and to their threats of what will happen if debts are not paid off—but suddenly, for all their power, they are finished. They no longer have teeth in their muzzles, they no longer catch prey, and their cubs wander away without food. That is how it goes with wealthy scoundrels: they are ruined under God's just hand—a well-deserved punishment. Every human being gets what he asks for.

4:12-21 THIS WAS CONFIRMED TO ME BY A VISION

I am no prophet but I, too, have sometimes had an experience that was very much like what happens to a prophet. Once, without anyone else noticing, a word of God stole in on me. I do not say that I understood it all. In the world of the divine, "inexpressible things" (2 Cor. 12:4) are heard, things of which I only understood a whisper. It was night and as I slept I perceived strange dream images. When I woke up and thought about them, I was seized with a nameless dread. Like a cool current of air a spirit, an envoy from the royal entourage of God (1 Kings 22:19-21), glided past me and, turning, stood before me. The hair on my body stood up on end from fear. I did not see much, only discerning a form standing in front of me. And like Elijah, the prophet of Israel (1 Kings 19:12), I heard a small voice that whispered to me: "No man can ever win a lawsuit against God; no man can ever appeal to his innocence before his Creator and so transfer his guilt to God. That is true even of God's highest creatures, the angels, who belong to his heavenly court and whom he sends out as messengers. He scrutinizes them and, if necessary, points out their mistakes. If this is true of God's 'mighty ones' (Ps. 103:20), then how much more of people, mere mortals, whose clay houses—their bodies—break down so easily. A man's foundations rest in, and are created of, the dust of the earth (Gen. 2:7). With a touch of exaggeration, it is easier to kill a man than a moth. A human being lives but for a day, exists only from the morning of life to life's evening. Really, his death causes no sensation in the heavenly courts above us. Just as a tent collapses the moment the cord is pulled out of the ground, so a human being collapses in a flash. In no way does a human being, not even at the end of this life, come to understand the meaning of his existence. It is useless to lodge a complaint against God." That is how the spectre spoke and confirmed the opinion I expressed a moment ago.

5:1-7 MISFORTUNE IS THE FRUIT OF WRONGDOING

You may call, if you wish, and request permission to institute legal proceedings over the misfortune inflicted on you, but no higher power will give it to you. None of the holy ones, members of the royal court, will take your case and enter a plea on your behalf against God. You only hasten your own death by pitting yourself, in annoyance and with such feeling, against God's arrangements. You are proving yourself a fool, unwise, falling short not only intellectually but also morally, for before the powers of heaven only silent submission is appropriate.

A person lacking in this submissiveness can perhaps prosper for a time, but all at once his fragile house of happiness collapses. I have seen this myself: a person who cared about neither God nor man prospered for a time but all at once it was all over with him. I could then refer to his case in imprecations: "May it go with the possessions of So-and-so as with the homestead of Mr. Fool!" He had enriched himself in the way I just described (4:8-11), but after his sudden death no one wanted to defend his children in court against the claimants he had injured and who demanded restitution (2 Kings 8:1-6). The young children in the case got the worst of it; in court others trampled on their claims to the property. They were not even able to keep the grain that had already been harvested. A group of hungry people, the ones who had been hurt by their father among them, simply took it, roasted some right on the spot, and carried the rest with them to their hovels. Mobs of poor devils just grabbed what they could of the possessions of the capitalist.

Misfortune, such as struck the rich fool, is not a product of nature, nor does it come up like weeds in a field, but is a part of a man's destiny. Being human, and so falling short in many ways, he must expect a good share of trouble and misery in life. Man is, and always has been, a sinner: misery is his element, as the blue yonder is of birds. Misfortune is the fruit of wrongdoing!

5:8-16 GOD CAN REVERSE MISFORTUNE

If I were in your shoes, I would not go to God with a complaint, which always implies some kind of accusation, but I would go to him with a request for advice and lay my cause before him: so do not indict him but await his judicial decision. You can trust God not only to give a verdict but also to put it into effect, for he can accomplish what no other being can. His mighty acts make all the difference in the lot of man and go far beyond all human calculations. Every day he performs innumerable wonders, things no man could do. You want an example, maybe? Look at the rain, necessary to our fields, but no man can force it out of the sky. By pouring down abundant rain on the fields of tenant farmers—who

35

possess no reserves of food or precious metal—God raises their existence, which first seemed precarious and miserable, to the heights of good fortune. Now they can reduce their burden of debt to the rich who, if the harvest had failed, were planning by legal means to take over the land of their debtors.

Those moneybags had such clever schemes! They would blithely have let the debt run up and loaned out grain for food and seed-grain for the following season—with a broad gesture of goodwill and with the thought of soon having the fields of the poor in their own hands. But God catches them in their own craftiness (1 Cor. 3:19): the same seed-grain bears abundant grain and enables the debtor to get the creditor off his back. The greedy lender had already pictured to himself what he would do with his new possession, but his plan proved to be premature: nothing comes of it. The man who, before, had nothing but debts, is rescued from the clutches of the rich. The man of capital fancied he, the lion, had the poor man between his teeth but when his jaws clamp shut there is nothing there. It was his purpose, by proper legal means of course, to commit moral injustice—robbing the poor farmer of his land—but now there is nothing he can lay his hands on. This is how God reverses misfortune!

5:17-27 THEN ALL WILL BE WELL AGAIN

God's blessings come on the heels of his corrections. Those corrections, however hard they may strike a person, are necessary: a person has to learn to acknowledge his utter dependence on God, but God does not stop at correction. By adversity he admonishes a man, like a father his children (Prov. 15:5). Notwithstanding the hard blows he sometimes inflicts, he is a gracious God who, provided the affliction has been rightly endured, will let greater blessings follow. He is no sadist who derives pleasure from another man's pain. Soon you will discover there is healing power in those hard hands of God.

That is how it will go with you also, Job. Let me for now use the "graduated numerical saying" of the wisdom teachers (cf. Prov. 30:15-31 [cf. Amos. 1:3–2:6]) to show how people are rescued by God from innumerable dangers:

1. In time of famine you do not starve to death.
2. In battle you escape the sword.

3. The slander of enemies does not hurt you.
4. They threaten to mistreat you but do not succeed.
5. Even if they do succeed and imprison you,
6. Without food, you are set free.
7. You need not even be afraid of the wild beasts, for God has subjected the entire animal kingdom to man (Gen. 1:28; Ps. 8:7-9).

That is how it goes with a person who takes God's corrections submissively to heart. That is how it will go with you if you can find the proper attitude under God's afflictions. Then your tent, your house and household, will be secure from misfortune. Your cattle and your grainfields will remain unaffected. Take my advice and you will find this to be true. You will live again like a patriarch with numerous descendants. You will reach a ripe old age in perfect health, and death, which is inevitable, will inspire no terror in you. As grain, ripened in the field and bound in sheaves, is gathered in the storehouse, so your children filled with gratitude will bring you to your final resting place. With eyes wide open, we have observed all this in the life of many a righteous person and learned the same things from the traditions of wisdom that the forefathers have handed down to us. As one of us, you have taught these things to others; now the important thing for you is to walk down the road of humble submission, which God is pointing out to you, yourself. Then all will be well again.

JOB'S ANSWER TO THE FIRST DISCOURSE OF ELIPHAZ 6:1–7:21

One must not attempt to find in Job's answer to Eliphaz a systematic refutation of his arguments. In a few places in chapter 6 Job reacts to what Eliphaz has said to him, but much in this chapter echoes his first complaint (chap. 3). In chapter 7 Job no longer addresses his friends at all; from verse 7 on he clearly addresses himself to God.

Like Eliphaz's discourse, Job's answer can be divided into six sections—and again the sections are of unequal length:

6:2-7	This is no comfort to me!
6:8-13	So I would rather die.
6:14-21	My friends have disappointed me.
6:22-30	They do not see that my case is exceptional.
7:1-10	My life is hard and short.
7:11-21	Why then pay so much attention to me?

In the first two sections Job pours out his complaint without speaking to anyone in particular; in the second pair he addresses himself to his friends in whose name Eliphaz has spoken; in the last two he addresses God.

6:2-7 THIS IS NO COMFORT TO ME!

What Eliphaz, speaking for all three, has said does not get to the bottom of my suffering. Take the balances, put into one bowl what I described in chapter 3 as my grievance, and into the other the pain into which I have been plunged. Then my misfortune will prove to be infinitely heavier than my well-justified complaint; it weighs on me with more weight than all the sand of the seashore. Is it any wonder I use words my friends think are rash? They just come storming out of me. I suffer physical and spiritual pain. God's arrows, sickness and misfortune, have pierced me; they are caught under my skin so that I cannot pull them out and the poison in the arrowheads makes my body sick and my spirit desperate. God's terrors, the most repulsive horrors, dreadful visions caused by fever, array themselves against me: I see their threatening forms before my eyes.

When an animal gets fodder that is to its taste, it makes no sounds of protest; it only brays or bellows when it finds nothing it can eat. What my friends, speaking through the mouth of Eliphaz, have served me in the way of comfort does not taste at all good to me. It was not "seasoned with salt" (Col. 4:6). It tasted to me like the slime of the purslane; the leaves and flowers may serve to ease the throat a little but the slime in the stems is awfully flat. This sort of "nourishment" just fills me with aversion; whatever vitality I have left in me rises up in rebellion in spite of my sickness. To put it plainly: I abhor such cheap words of consolation. They are no comfort to me at all.

6:8-13 SO I WOULD RATHER DIE

My only hope is a speedy death. Would that the Lord of life and death fulfilled this hope! If only he were so kind as to give me that final blow. I am a weaving on a loom (cf. Ps. 139:13); let my life now be considered complete. As far as I am concerned, God is free to cut the threads of the warp. It would be a relief even if it hurt for a moment. To me it would come as a deliverance. All I ask of God is the grace of death— my reward for the fact that in my life I have so often preached God's word to others; the thing that you, Eliphaz, cited against me a minute ago (4:3-4).

Life has nothing left to offer me. My strength is gone and there is no point in my still waiting, in pain and misery, for a reversal of fortune. It will never come. I am so close to death that it makes no sense to wait patiently for a turn of events such as Eliphaz pictured (5:17-26). It might be different if I were young and still full of vitality, but now all prospect of success is gone. So I would rather die.

6:14-21 MY FRIENDS HAVE DISAPPOINTED ME

They did come; they sat with me in silence for seven days, but now that one of them has begun to speak it is evident that they wish to dispose of me with pious talk. Although they sit here with me, and although they try to put fresh heart in me, for all their talk, they leave me in the lurch and they are lacking in true piety. I dreamed in vain that they would refresh me as with a drink of water from a clear-flowing brook. They put me in mind of a winter brook that, fed by melting ice and snow, rushes down rapidly and with much water, but dries out when the winter season is past. For a time a few thin ribbons of water still flow sluggishly through the channels but soon they smother in the banks of sand that winter has deposited.

Then, when a caravan comes from afar, say from Tema, an oasis on the ancient caravan route connecting the Persian Gulf with the Gulf of Aqaba, or from Sheba on the southern coast of Arabia, the travelers figure they can replenish their water supply at the brook, but the water is gone, the stream is dry. That is how it is with my friends: in the days of my prosperity their friendship seemed very promising; but now

seeing me in hot distress, they leave me to myself. I ache for
real sympathy but they do not really enter into my suffering.
They look at me as someone afflicted by God and find it safest
to stand on the side of God. They are afraid to become involved in the horror of my lot. They have disappointed me.

6:22-30 THEY DO NOT SEE THAT MY CASE IS EXCEPTIONAL

Although I have been stripped of all I had, I myself have never
held up my hand like a beggar for a handout. I have never
laid violent hands on anyone's life or limbs, a crime for which
I would have had to pay a high ransom, and have not called
on you to help me pay it out of your resources. I never took
out a mortgage on my property so that now, having been
robbed of everything, I would have to beg you for a financial
contribution to help me face a ruthless creditor. I never fell
into the slavery of debt at the hands of inhuman capitalists
and so I do not have to ask if you would perhaps buy my
freedom.

The only thing I ask for is words of genuine sympathy.
I do not understand my life-situation; if you will help me
understand it, I will listen attentively. If in any respect I have
erred—perhaps unconsciously—then make it clear to me by
a concrete reference to my failure.

What I have said came out of a heart that is genuinely
confused and perplexed. By putting that confusion into words
I did not injure you, did I? Your corrections do not help me
at all; they only push me deeper into the dirt. The issue after
all is not what I have said or my choice of words; the issue is
the incomprehensible suffering that has come over me. It is
not right to squelch the cries of a despairing man, such as I,
with a passing remark or with some general statement of wisdom. Really, it is no small matter when someone prays or
begs for death to come; one may not take it lightly and counter
it with a few everyday statements of wisdom. In no respect
have I been able to tell that you take seriously the intolerable
burden that has been laid on me. Really to suffer *with* someone—of that you have no idea. If some orphan were left a
wretched estate, you as creditors would cast lots to see which
of you would take the child in possession as a slave (cf. 2 Kings
4:1). If a friend of yours were in debt to you, you would not

only deprive him of his freedom by making him a slave—you would even (against the intent of Exod. 21:1-11) sell him to the international slavetraders (cf. Neh. 5:8).

So stop reasoning so abstractly and pay attention to my exceptional case—the kind of attention one has a right to expect from genuine friends. All I have said, and will continue to say, is no more than the appalling truth that I, without having committed any sin against God or my fellow human beings, have been thrust into unbearable misfortune. You do me an injustice by supposing that in some fashion or other I have deserved this misfortune. Let go of that attitude! Again: *let go* of that attitude! Even though in my perplexity I tend to express myself in strong words, I am completely right in my complaints. I have not said a word too many; one cannot take my words ill of me. Just as one's palate infallibly registers a bitter taste, so do I know all too well the taste of disaster. I am not dealing with theoretical questions; in my own body and spirit I experience undeserved suffering. You, however, do not see the exceptional character of my case.

7:1-10 MY LIFE IS HARD AND SHORT

I will no longer talk with you: my dispute is with God, the God who lets human beings toil on earth under heavy burdens of labor and pain that have been laid on them unasked. Like the existence of a day laborer, from whom employers exact the utmost while it is day, so—to speak, too, for a moment in general terms—is my life and that of the likes of me. While he toils, the slave has but one wish: that it may soon be evening and dark so that work has to stop. The day laborer waits with longing for the moment when, after the sun has gone down, his meager wage will be paid out to him (cf. Lev. 19:13; Deut. 24:15; Matt. 20:8). With me it is worse: this illness of mine may drag on for months—and to what purpose? There is no prospect of wages to sweeten my term of service. Even at night I find no rest. When it is time to sleep, the sleep that might drug me will not come, and I want to get up again: perhaps another position will bring relief. So I lie now on one side, then on the other, and get tired of all my tossing and turning; this continues till morning twilight. Then I see my body again—how hideous! Maggots infest my sores in one place and in another pus and dirt have united to form crusts.

41

Under the swellings I can see my blood vessels pump; the tumors break open and fester.

Therefore God, you who brought all this upon me, please remember that my life races to the end. It will soon be past and there is nothing good I am still waiting for. You are called a God who sees people (Gen. 16:13), but soon there will be no Job anymore. Then you will turn your gaze on me, but there will be no "me" to see, not even to your all-seeing eye. Once a person has died he does not return to the land of the living, any more than a cloud returns after it has faded away into the blue. The dead man does not return to his family; no one who knew him will meet him again (Ps. 103:16). My life is hard and short.

7:11-21 WHY THEN PAY SO MUCH ATTENTION TO ME?

If this, then, be so—and for me in my grief and sickness at least it is so—I am entitled to say exactly what I think and to pour out all the anguish of my heart. It will be good for you, God, to hear how bitter you have made things for me. And why did you? I am no danger to the world-order, am I? I am not like the sea at the time of creation (cf. 38:8-11), or like Leviathan, the Chaos monster (cf. 3:8), am I? One would almost think I was, considering how you restrict me and rob me of freedom. You allow me not a moment's rest. When at last sleep comes mercifully over my body, you make sure that I will still be troubled: feverish visions pursue me and I wake up out of terrifying nightmares. If only I were strangled and my breath and life were cut off. I would rather die than be able any longer to feel with my fingers the ribs under my wasted flesh (cf. Ps. 22:17). I am mortal, am I not? My life is already busily flowing away. Leave me alone, then, so that I can go in peace. You do not have to fear that I will do anything against you; an entire human life, compared with your eternal existence, is really nothing.

There is not the least reason to pay so much attention to a person (Ps. 8:5). He is a most insignificant little part of your creation. Why then do you keep coming back to him to see if he is keeping his affairs in order? Why lay such heavy burdens on him? Is it to experiment with him to see how long he can keep it up? Please give me a moment of respite from your uninvited attention, and let me come to! Are you afraid that I will break some commandment of yours? Suppose I did—what injury would you suffer? It would not threaten your eternal omnipotence, would it? People praise you for being a faithful watchman over your flock (Ps. 80:1), but I have had more than enough of your attention. You are an eternal nagger rather than a good shepherd!

It seems I always have to be the target for your arrows. Don't you ever get tired of always aiming them at me? Would it not be much easier for you simply to ignore my possible missteps—if there are any? Can you never let anything pass? All that fuss is completely unnecessary—before you know it I will be in my grave and turn into dust. Then you will look for me—perhaps to aim another arrow at me or perhaps to do something to make up for all the injustice you have done me— but then there will be nothing left for you to do. Job will be gone! Then why pay so much attention to me?

BILDAD'S FIRST DISCOURSE 8:1-22

Job's second friend begins to speak. Impatient with Job's reply to Eliphaz, he is somewhat harsher than the first speaker. There is in Bildad's argumentation, more than in the discourse of Eliphaz, a suspicion that in the days of Job's prosperity he has committed certain sins, whatever they may have been, and that he is now being punished by God for them.

Bildad's discourse can be divided into three sections of practically equal length:

8:2-7   Not protest but conversion is needed.
8:8-15   That is what the experience of previous gen-
           erations teaches us.
8:16-22   The prosperity of the godless is temporary.

Bildad's first discourse is noticeably much shorter than that of Eliphaz. The same is true of his second and, especially, his third discourse. As a rule Job's replies are much longer than his friends' admonitions.

8:2-7 NOT PROTEST BUT CONVERSION IS NEEDED

A person who protests against his suffering incurs the displeasure of God and man. The things that you, Job, have said so far arouse only the impatience of the listener. You hurl one indictment against God after another; your words storm against him. But you yourself have to admit it is inconceivable that God himself would deviate from the paths of justice and fairness that he has laid down for us human beings. So the death of your children, Job, must be the outcome of their transgressions, even though you and we do not know what sins they have committed. Evil is its own punishment (cf. Jer. 2:19). God does not even have to take special measures against a sinner; he simply needs to turn the evildoer over to his own wickedness and it will ruin him. It is enough for God to withdraw his hand from him—to leave him to the power of his sin.

That is how it was with your children: at their feasts they evidently forgot about God. Now that is also a lesson for you. You are still alive and have a chance to better yourself. You must take advantage of it; that is, take up contact anew with the God who has abandoned you. Repent of your self-righteousness, the self-righteousness that comes through in your protests; and do not beg God for justice but for mercy. Such repentance requires a pure heart and an upright walk of life; if they are present in your case, then God will take up your cause. It appears now as if he is sleeping; he obviously does not do a thing, and has left you in the power of your sin. But if you come to him in humility, with a sincere plea, he will rouse himself, intervene, and restore you to your "place"— your previous state as the father of a large family and the owner of great possession. Your repentance entitles you to it, for he rewards those who seek him diligently (cf. Heb. 11:6). In fact, he will do more than only restore you to your former state: he will bless you so generously that your former happiness will seem small by comparison with what you will receive then.

8:8-15 THAT IS WHAT THE EXPERIENCE OF PREVIOUS GENERATIONS TEACHES US

Eliphaz appealed to a divine revelation that came to him; I will place alongside of that the traditional wisdom of previous generations, which came to the same conclusions on the basis of their experience. You will do well to inquire into it. Our own life on earth is a passing shadow and our personal experience only covers a short period of time—not more than the day of yesterday, so to speak. So it makes sense to figure not only with your own experience but especially with that of preceding generations. The wisdom of centuries has been distilled in the proverbs handed down to us (e.g., in Ps. 37), proverbs that are full of a wisdom you should now apply to yourself.

We can make the same point with the aid of examples derived from nature. It is only in the marshes at the northernmost sources of the Jordan that papyrus can really grow tall; it is only along the muddy banks of rivers that reeds luxuriate. Why should that be? It is because of the abundance of water that is available to them in such places, and water is for such plants what God's blessing is for man. The seeds of such vegetation naturally also fall in places other than marshland or river bottoms and there it will also start to grow, moist as the soil may still be from winter rains and snow. But before long the ground dries out, even before the plants are tall enough to be cut as fodder for the cattle; and whereas other kinds of grass still have months of growth ahead of them, the shoots of papyrus and reeds wither in a few days.

That is how it goes with all those who fail to cultivate contact with God in their life. They think there is no end to their wealth (cf. Ps. 49:12), but again: evil is its own punishment. The person who stops seeking God in humble prayer can only expect evil. Since so far all his undertakings have prospered, he begins to trust his own business acumen and his own well-placed investments. But what do all these clever schemes amount to? They are fragile as autumn threads that cannot hold a person, bits of a spider's web that offer no security when the bottom of one's riches drops out from beneath us. No more can one lean on one's family—younger brothers or sons—for they all collapse with us.

8:16-22 THE PROSPERITY OF THE GODLESS IS TEMPORARY

Such newly rich people sometimes make you think of succulent plants with runners, like pumpkins or melons. It is astonishing the way their runners creep over the ground and spread out and soon cover the whole garden, regardless of what other, smaller plants may be in the way. In a far corner of the garden you have piled up the stones that surfaced when you were digging, but our pumpkins pay no attention to that at all—they send out their runners over, and even in between, them. In the same way an unprincipled capitalist knows how to profit even from a time of recession. But the time comes when the gardener has had enough of it; he throws all that wild growth onto a rubbish heap and the garden no longer shows a trace of the usurper. With a sigh of relief it says: "I never had any dealings with it!" and, in any case, from that moment on it will have no truck with it. Similarly, the joy of the unjust rich man is only temporary and from the perspective of its catastrophic ending it hardly deserves to be called "joy," for financial ruin makes the memory of previous prosperity feel bitter. Just as weeds come up out of the soil without any help from anyone, so a new crop of speculators soon arrives on the scene, but their fate will be no different.

A man of integrity, who does not try to enrich himself in devious ways, does not have to fear such a judgment. God does not begrudge him a place in his garden, nor reject him— nor will he reject you, Job, if at least you are such a man. If you are not, you must not count on anything, for God extends no help to evildoers. But we shall assume for the moment that you are not guilty of those practices. Well, then, soon you will be able to laugh again; soon you will be able to enjoy life again; and those who have turned away from you in your state of misfortune will shrink away in shame. There is just no stability in the "tents"—in the lives across the board—of people who allow themselves a range of evil acts and bad faith. One moment they are on top of the heap, the next they are nothing.

JOB'S ANSWER TO BILDAD'S FIRST DISCOURSE 9:1–10:22

We can divide Job's answer to Bildad's discourse into five sections, again of unequal length, but all of them containing approximately twelve verses. While in his reply to Eliphaz Job addressed three parts of his discourse to his friend and three to his God, in his reply to Bildad he switches to direct address

to God earlier in his discourse, so that only two of the five
sections are addressed to Bildad.

We wish to characterize these five sections as follows:

9:2-13   True: no one can succeed in opposing God.
9:14-24   I give up arguing with him.
9:25-35   For an honest debate one needs a referee.
10:1-12   God does not destroy his own work, does he?
10:13-22   It would be better if you had not created me.

9:2-13 TRUE: NO ONE CAN SUCCEED
IN OPPOSING GOD

I have discovered through rather bitter experience that God
can suddenly bring about a total change in a person's life.
And if it is a change for the worse, it does not help to maintain
one's own right before God. Even if one is right, the real issue
is to be put in the right, and for that one does not get a chance
with God. If God should opt, for whatever reason or for no
reason at all, to assume the role of an adversary against a man,
then that man could not give an adequate answer even to one
out of a thousand accusing questions. All that God says remains in effect—and whatever a person says against it may
make sense to that person but it has no effect at all. Against
that combination of wisdom and omnipotence a person is
helpless. Perhaps for a moment a person might risk opposing
him, but that is an exercise in recklessness. A human being
only has words at his disposal; God strikes as it suits him.

One should take the time to picture to himself the sorts
of things God does! Mountains, which make a person feel so
little, are ravaged by him—especially in the limestone mountain area where I live, where subterranean streams cause the
formation of caves that suddenly collapse; it happens so quickly
that even if the mountains were conscious, they would not
know who it was that was turning against them so disturb-
ingly. Sometimes the earth shakes beneath our feet; it may
seem to be thoroughly attached to the mountains, the pillars
of the earth, which give to it a semblance of stability; but the
opposite proves to be true when God stages an earthquake.
Even the sun, which is so powerful—much mightier than our
earth—is subject to God's arrangements, and sometimes it
disappears from sight, when the sky is darkened by very bad

weather or by sandstorms. The same thing happens to the stars at night: it is as if God covers them up and seals the cover.

There is no denying that the entire cosmos is the work of his hands; he alone, without help from anyone, stretched out the heavens like an immense tent over our heads. The sea with its high-cresting waves by no means limits his freedom of movement. He is the Creator of the constellations and has absolute rule over them; they are not independent, neither the Bear nor the enormous constellation of Orion nor that little accumulation of stars we call the Pleiades, the seven stars in the Taurus constellation. For the stars we see in summer, but not in winter, God has prepared chambers in the south, far below the horizon, where they "hibernate." In short, the creation is full of wonders we cannot fathom or even add up, and it is only his activity that sets it all in motion.

And if then we turn, in bedazzlement, back to ourselves, we discover that his actions with people are just as incomprehensible. If he is about to do something with a person, he may pass within inches of that person but the person, in his small circle, does not even notice it, not even to mention the possibility of keeping God from coming too close. If God were planning to rob a person of anything, as he did when he snatched away my children and my possessions, there is not one who could stop him, not even to call him to account with the question "What are you doing?" If he has it in mind to strike or judge a person, we humans speak of his wrath, but the "why" and "wherefore" of that wrath remain a mystery to us, let alone that we with our human logic could persuade him not to carry out his plan. Rahab, the recalcitrant material we so often run into, with its heroic helpers, the powers inherent in matter, bow helplessly, like defeated enemies, under his feet and are completely subject to him.

9:14-24 I GIVE UP ARGUING WITH HIM

But if cosmic powers are powerless before him, what can I do? Call him to account? Enter the fray against him with choice words and arguments? It could be that in my own eyes I would have a lawful complaint but against such an opponent words are useless. I would soon discover that I had to change tactics: no longer indict him but, as though I were the accused, beg for mercy—and so acknowledge his right to do as he pleases. Suppose I called for justice and he responded—that would be so unlikely that I could not believe he took my protest seriously.

Like a thundercloud, his judgment hangs over my head; at any moment the lightning may strike—and that is exactly what happens! Just look at the wounds he has multiplied, wounds to my body, wounds to my soul; and all that without telling me why he is hurting me so. And this just goes on; he does not give me a moment of respite. I just have to swallow whatever he decides to inflict on me, bitter though it is. If we compare his strength with mine, he is the giant who cries out in battle "Look out!" or "Come here if you dare!" as though he were challenging a dwarf. If the issue is who is right, it turns out he stands above the law; he will not let himself be summoned before a judge.

Suppose I could summon him—at his appearance my confusion would be so intense, whatever I stammered out could be used against me. I could insist that I have always been blameless in my behavior, but before such a court and against such an adversary I would still be vanquished. I would talk myself into a corner and be indicted as a swindler, un-masked, and not let go. I may stand by my conviction that I am a man of integrity, but in the contest with God I would lose in any case, and so forfeit my life; for a person who accuses God touches his majesty and risks a sentence of death.

But even now how does my life differ from a slow death? Certainly, a death sentence is no worse than the state I am in now. It all comes down to the same thing and so, fully aware of the risks I am running, I utter the pronouncement: God treats the best and the worst alike: he destroys both. Just consider what happens when an epidemic, like a scourge in the hand of God, strikes a population. All at once there are an enormous number of deaths and no questions are asked about good or evil conduct: the judgment of death mocks all moral qualities. Those who have never done evil either to God or to man despair of God's justice, they melt away as it were in their desperation, but God remains completely unmoved.

Isn't this true in general and under all circumstances? Are not the mightiest men on earth those who stop at neither injustice nor violence? And are not the judges accustomed to act as if they know nothing of it? Does not God blindfold them so that they perceive no injustice in those who govern? God—yes, *God*—is the cause of these wretched conditions. If he is not, then what is he? A God who cannot rule the world? A God who is blind to injustice? Are not all things that happen on earth the effects of his will? God would not be worth the title "God" if it were different.

9:25-35 FOR AN HONEST DEBATE ONE NEEDS A REFEREE

Like every human life, so mine rushes past like a runner with a message, who does not rest till he has delivered it at its destination. Nowhere does he stop to rest; similarly, my life hastens on, without pause, to its destination: death. On the stream of life I skim past like boats of papyrus on the Nile. On air currents high in the sky the eagle soars without flapping a wing, till he swoops down on the carrion on which he feeds. So I circle around without doing a thing and soon I will swoop down on my prey, death.

I can make up my mind to forget my misery, act as if I am a soul without cares, smooth away my wrinkles, and put a good face on a bad game, but before I can put my intention into effect, I become very aware of the pain and misery of my illness, and perceive that God treats me as a criminal who deserves this punishment. That is the worst part: that I cannot obtain justice from the God who tortures me. You, God, are the judge in your own case; no wonder I am put in the wrong. There is no point in accusing God in God's court. No matter how I plead for myself, my experience is like that of a person who washes himself with crystal-clear water in the creeks that run down from snow-covered mountains, and on top of that uses washing soda, the best detergent there is; the moment I think I am clean he tosses me into a mudhole, so that my clothes, which I took off before taking my bath, begin to stink from the new dirt that is on my body. If they could speak they would say: "We loathe touching that man's body!"

With a human adversary I would know what to do: I would summon him before a court to start an honest trial. But there is no one who can arbitrate between a man and God; no one can assert his authority over both, prevent the stronger from overpowering the weaker, and keep him from attacking the weaker one bodily with his rod or silence him with threats.

If only such a judge could be found! Then I could indict God without fear of consequences, for if I forget but for a moment that I am dealing with God and not with a man, then justice is clearly on my side. If I look only at myself, my conduct and personality, I have not the slightest reason to fear that the verdict would not be in my favor.

10:1-12 GOD DOES NOT DESTROY HIS OWN WORK, DOES HE?

What remains of my life is so wretched that I could not care less for it. Therefore, though I know that by speaking out against God I will lose my life, I do not care anymore. I do not want to live any longer; I only want to utter what is in my heart to say. Even if every complaint turns out to be an accusation—an accusation against God, who can react to it with a sentence of death—my bitterness must be uttered. And so I say to God: Please do not begin by condemning me before I know why. Don't I have a right to know what you have against me? Let me hear at last what you are charging me with; then we can talk.

What is there in it for you, trampling on everything that counts as just among men, to mistreat me so? I have not made myself; it is your hands that have created me. Do you despise your own handiwork? And do you let your light shine on people who are really guilty and do you favor them with happiness in spite of their evil intentions, while I am thrust out in the darkness? If you were a man, I would understand. Men are often mistaken in their judgment or are unable to separate their own interest from it. But you, the eternal God, do not have to be afraid, do you, that I, a mortal man whose life is brief, will do you lasting harm? I cannot compete with you; why then do you deem it necessary to watch me all the time to see if I will make a misstep? Say I did make a misstep— which is not the case—would I offend your omnipotence by it? You can always do with me as you please—now can't you?

You have caused me to be born and made me what I was—healthy and whole. But now you are tearing up your own artwork; now you are devouring me as if you were a monster. It would be well if you remembered that I have been molded by you, the way a bowl is molded by a potter: it is all your own work and no threat to you, for soon enough the

51

bowl will break and turn to dust. Was it not under your rule that my father poured his semen into the womb of my mother? Was it not under your rule that the semen, like milk at the cheesemaker's, curdled and became an embryo in the uterus? It became skin and flesh; bones and tendons grew, like a piece of knitting or weaving (Ps. 139:13). You gave me life—and what a life! Every day I experienced your love and faithfulness. You took care that no illness or accident got to me in those days—days that now seem to lie so far behind me, for everything has turned into its opposite.

10:13-22 IT WOULD BE BETTER IF YOU HAD NOT CREATED ME

You had some purpose in mind with me, a purpose of which I had not the slightest inkling in the time of my prosperity but that has finally come home to me in my suffering. It was this: always to watch me and to exploit even the least peccadillo that I might perhaps, without knowing it, commit, as an excuse to take a position against me.

And now the situation is this: if I really did deserve punishment, well, I get the very worst. But if I am right in protesting, then I still cannot raise my head and claim my rights, for I am an outcast, despised by God and man, and an example of how much misery may come over a person. Even if I were to raise my head in my present lost condition, then you would still begrudge me my sense of self-worth and fall on me like a lion pouncing on his prey, and again let that incomprehensible and unlimited power of yours loose on me, in order, if that were possible, to torture me even more. As though you were a prosecutor in a courtroom, you call for fresh witnesses against me over and over and come with new charges against me. The content of the charges keeps changing: instead of some supposed crime I have committed, the charge is now that I am proud, and the term of hard labor to which I am sentenced only gets extended. It would have been better for me had I never been born or had I been stillborn. In the latter case it would have been as if I had never lived in my mother's womb. Then I would have been carried, without a name, directly from the womb to the grave. I do not have much longer to live and you can safely avert your attention from me. That will entail no risks for you at all. Allow me a few days of rest before I go; favor me with a moment in which to put a smile on my face. For soon I will go to the kingdom of the dead, the land from which no traveler returns, where all is darkness, so that a man cannot tell one person from another—the kingdom from which all rank has been removed and where even the light is pitch-dark, so to speak. There I will not trouble you nor you me.

ZOPHAR'S FIRST DISCOURSE 11:1-20

Like Bildad's first discourse, so that of the third friend is much shorter than that of Eliphaz. It is distinguished from those of the first two friends by the fact that it is more of a response to what Job has said in his answer to them. For that reason it is considerably more agressive, addressing what Job says rather than what he is or was.

In Zophar's discourse we can distinguish two parts:

11:2-12   No man knows God's secrets.
11:13-20   The prayer of a righteous man is powerful and effective.

11:2-12 NO MAN KNOWS GOD'S SECRETS

You have much to say about God, my friend Job, but that long stream of words is easy to refute. A refutation just has to be offered or else you might even begin to think that both God and man would agree with you for no other reason than that you talk so incessantly. Anyone with a little intelligence will refuse to be impressed by such a river of nonsense. We have heard how you tried to overwhelm God with your mockery, but we shall still bring you around to an attitude of shame and repentance.

You claim that there is nothing wrong with what you have said of God and that not just your words but your entire life is free from sin. I assume you are sincere about that, but that is only your own human judgment. It would be very different if we could hear God talk about Job, instead of hearing Job about God. In fact, I could wish, in your own interest, that God would now begin to speak and make it very clear to you, once and for all, that a person cannot speak about him the way you do. He would then proceed to give you some insight into the mysteries of his wisdom—the motives for his actions, motives that are incomprehensible to human beings. That would be profitable for you and teach you God's wisdom in addition to that of man. You would then discover that God has not even given you what you deserve in the way of punishment, and that God has chosen to overlook much of your wrongdoing against him.

It is true: God still keeps silent and that is why I now have to speak up for him. Therefore I have to ask you, Job: Do you extend your scrutiny to God? Have you any idea why he does what he does? You said that you knew God's secret purpose against you (10:13-14)—but have you really reached the point where you have knowledge of God's secrets, and have you understood them to the limit? For then you would have to rise higher than the vault of heaven—and discover your powerlessness. You would have to dig deeper than the realm of the dead under the earth—and confess your ignorance. You could more easily traverse the entire earth and cross the breadth of the sea than survey the width of God's government of the world. Reflect for a moment on that height, that depth, that length, and that width (cf. Eph. 3:18) and you will realize that, for us human beings before God, only silent acceptance of his unfathomable will is appropriate.

Should he come along and relate actively to human beings, and give some over to death and keep others with him on earth—who is in a position, and who would even dare, to protest? God knows who are false and worthless and whose lives are hollow—are mere sham. He does not have to hold lengthy inquiries to find out: all things lie open and uncovered before him (cf. Heb. 4:13). He really does not have to hunt, as you claimed (10:6), to find our sins. Humans, about whose procreation and birth you have so much to say (10:9-11), are actually hollow inside, without backbone or content, like a badly baked cake, all crust and nothing inside! He is born an ass, even as the colt of a wild ass, the kind you cannot tame and always keeps dashing off. How could such a being judge God's government of the universe?

11:13-20 THE PRAYER OF A RIGHTEOUS MAN IS POWERFUL AND EFFECTIVE

Instead of offering criticism it would be much better to position your inner self in the opposite direction: lift up your

hands, palms up and fingers outstretched to God as a peti-
tioner, in order to ask him humbly like a beggar for redemp-
tion from misery. But, remember! Those hands must be clean.
There must not be unjust gain in them. If there is anything
anywhere in your household that has been obtained by unlawful means, remove that first. When *that* has been done,
you can approach God, pure and righteous, without stain of
sin. Then you will be in a strong position, like a metal casting,
and need not be afraid of God's retributive justice.

Even though great misery has come upon you, once you
have eliminated all unrighteousness from your existence, you
need not trouble yourself over your suffering. It will pass;
after a while you can think of it as of a flood that for a short
time filled the river bottom but is now gone and has left it
traversable again. True, now you sit in darkness but the darkness of the realm of the dead, which you earlier described so
terrifyingly (10:21-22), will soon recede far from you. Life will
soon blossom for you again and smile at you, like the sun at
its zenith. And when the sun goes down, and it is evening,
then that is only a harbinger of the new day that will shine
on you. As a prophet has said (Isa. 58:10): "If you pour yourself out for the hungry and satisfy the desire of the afflicted,
then shall your light rise in the darkness and your gloom shall
be as the noonday." Or with the words of another prophet
(Zech. 14:7): ". . . at evening time there shall be light."

Then, when you pray to God as a righteous man, you no
longer need to complain, as you did in your answer to Eliphaz
(7:6), that "your days come to an end without hope." You can
then expect every kind of blessing from God and rely on them.
The night will no longer haunt you with the terrors of men
or of God, very differently from what you described to Eliphaz
(7:14), namely, that God frightened you with dreams and terrified you with visions. And once you have put your affairs
in order with God, your relations with people, too, will im-
prove. You will regain your old position of honor. But don't
forget: it is only the prayer of the *righteous* man that is powerful and effective. Watch that you will not have to be counted
among the scoundrels who cause injury to other people from
a desire for their own gain; their fate is very different. What
they have to look forward to is very drab—devoid of joy.
When judgment falls on their sinful existence there will be no

place of refuge for them, either with God or men. The only thing they can look forward to is death.

JOB'S ANSWER TO ZOPHAR'S FIRST DISCOURSE 12:1–14:22

It immediately strikes the reader that Job's answer to Zophar is much longer than his answers to Eliphaz and Bildad. The last two encompass fifty-one and fifty-seven verses respectively; but his answer to Zophar extends over three chapters, seventy-five verses in all. It is hard to discover a reason for this. One might suppose that since this is Job's answer to the last of his three friends, an attempt was made to round off the cycle, as when at the end of the third round Job continues to speak six chapters in duration (26–31); but from 27:1 on we have a new division in which Job does not address himself to his friends again. Furthermore, at the conclusion of the second cycle, Job's answer to Zophar is not exceptionally long.

It has been suggested that in the present subdivision some sections, such as 12:4-12, are later interpolations, or perhaps parts of the original work that in the course of time have been moved from their proper location. But this is not self-evident; we find nothing in 12:4-12 that could not be the work of the original poet, nor can we point to a better location for the passage. For these reasons we shall hold to the text as it has been handed down, and admit that we cannot say why in this case it is so long.

As always we shall divide Job's discourse in a number of sections of unequal length:

12:2-13	Human wisdom cannot fathom the ways of God.
12:14-25	God overthrows all our certainties.
13:1-12	Stop looking for arguments in defense of God.
13:13-19	Rather listen to what I have to say to God.
13:20-28	At least if God is prepared to respond in reason.
14:1-12	A person only lives once, and that only for a short time.
14:13-22	God does not give a person a second chance.

12:2-13 HUMAN WISDOM CANNOT FATHOM THE WAYS OF GOD

You are the representatives of prevailing popular views and, indeed, in your opposition to my expressed grievances against God, you have shown yourself to be the very pillars of established society. Moreover, you are convinced that no one can interpret the current wisdom better than you; you self-indulgently suppose that, if you were to die, wisdom would no longer enjoy such eloquent advocates. But I am not a whit less intelligent than you; I, too, can line up pretty arguments and assert that, in God's government and the course of human life, everything is in order. And not I alone! Every normal human being can put such "profundities" on display.

But we are not talking about the world in general; we are talking about my personal situation, and that is this: Here is a man who for no reasons known to him has been plunged into such deep misery that he has become a laughingstock among his acquaintances. His fellowmen say or think: "He will not listen to us; he keeps speaking to God—well then, let God answer him!" And all this they say when it is precisely my complaint that God does not reply to my protests. You righteous and proper people, enjoying your prosperity and good health without letup, you can talk so easily, but to my ears your talk sounds like mockery of my suffering. From a person's ill-fortune you infer his sin, the alleged cause of it, and so you only feel contempt for me as sinner, who gets what he deserves. Of course, for such an attitude as yours a sacred text can easily be found (Ps. 15:4), which says that in the eyes of the righteous a vile man is despised. Ill-fortune, you think, is simply the fate of those who have not strictly kept to the path of virtue. But what is the reality that demonstrates itself a hundred times over in this life? Robbers, who fatten themselves at the expense of their fellowmen, live untroubled in their dwellings. By violating the social laws of God they provoke him, but God chooses not to pay attention to it. It is he who not only favors them with a privileged position in society, but also gives them the opportunity to abuse their position. Therefore it is mistaken logic to attribute the misery of the oppressed and the brutalized to sins they have possibly committed before misfortune came upon them.

That is true not only in human society; we find the same

thing in all of nature. You could question the dumb animals. Oxen are put to hard labor, hitched to plow or wagon, and when they get too old they are butchered for their hide or meat. Have they asked for this fate? Have they committed any sins? It is only a superior power that decrees this cruel fate. Similarly with the birds: they flit through the air as though they were free, but a man hits them with some projectile and they drop to the ground. It is no different with the earth: I mean the creatures that live in the earth—worms and such. You turn the soil over and cut the worm in two; there is neither meaning nor profit in it for you but it happens. Fish are pulled by hook or net out of their element and lie helplessly gasping for air on the dry land. Does the fisherman first ask which have been the good and which the evil fish?

All these things proclaim the same message: the Creator of the world has so arranged it that the strong and the clever can do to the weak and the simple whatever comes to their mind. Whatever lives owes its existence to God and he does with it what he wants. As a prophet has said (Isa. 41:20): ". . . the hand of the Lord has done this." He has all power and we cannot bind him to our moral standards. We cannot account for his behavior and he gives no account of it to us.

I cannot help the fact that I have to reject your arguments. A person who eats food can tell immediately if something tastes good to him or not; he cannot change his taste. Just so, when I listen to your arguments, I immediately sense that they do not tally with the experience of my life. That is not a matter of faultfinding on my part: it is a spontaneous reaction.

You men, old and venerable as you are, have much to say to me, but the point is not how old and venerable you are, but how true or untrue your arguments are. Life in general, but particularly my own life, is not the least bit clarified by what you have to say. I can only tell that you do not understand the course of my life any more than I do. God—indeed, *God*—knows why he has done these things to me; his wisdom and his omnipotence coincide—which is exactly why we do not understand even a fraction of what he does.

12:14-25 GOD OVERTHROWS ALL OUR CERTAINTIES

God works not only positively as Creator, but also negatively as Destroyer, and he cannot be resisted as Destroyer any more than as Creator. When he tears down our walls of defense, we cannot rebuild them. If he then turns the people, now defenseless, over into the enslaving hands of their enemies, they cannot set themselves free. That is how it goes in nature: when at God's command the rain stops coming down, the brooks run dry; and if, after a long drought, the showers finally start coming again, they erode the fields. So both drought and rainfall are fatal to us. Again: he can do literally anything and knows how to put his plans into effect. If it seems to him desirable he gives to some the skill to mislead their fellow human beings into follies of all kinds, and from those fellowmen he takes away the intellects to see through the deception.

Human power and human wisdom—what can they do against God's counsel and plan? There go the professional wise men, members of the royal council, without their robes of office, led away by the enemy in their underclothing as slaves. There sit the judges who have to make pronouncements on complicated cases: they are not going to solve them anymore. The fate of the priests is like that of the members of council: they are taken captive and await a slave's life. Then you have the "well-fixed," wealthy citizens, now broadly sitting on their assets—indeed, but they will come tumbling down. At a time of catastrophe the "pillars" of the throne, those loyal protectors of the state, have not a word to say; the members of the senate no longer see a way out. Scions of ancient families are covered with mockery by the conquerors and, as a symbol of their powerlessness, their belts are undone and their clothes hang loose. They can no longer act with authority.

It is like a landslip: the upper layers of the ground slide away and the layers that lay hidden in the dark underneath come to the surface. What for? To what purpose? In the same way God allows huge landslips to occur in the history of nations. For a time a given tribe flourishes and expands—only because God so orders it—and, next, the same tribe is struck by a catastrophe and disappears—again because God so orders it. Human policies cannot prevent it or stop it: the rulers are at their wit's end and wander witlessly around like lost travelers in the wilderness, or like people overtaken by nightfall, or like drunkards who cannot find their way home. All that seemed to be certain has disappeared.

13:1-12 STOP LOOKING FOR ARGUMENTS IN DEFENSE OF GOD

I have seen God as the great Destroyer also in my own life; and I have heard the stories of earlier generations. Again (cf. 12:3): I am not less intelligent than you; anyone with eyes in his head can see these things. But even though I expanded on that subject for a moment to show that I can testify, just as eloquently as you can, to what experience and tradition have taught me, I really did not want to address myself to you. My quarrel is not with you but with God. You want to act as his defenders, but there are cracks in the structure of the world that you want "to plaster shut," as a prophet has said (Ezek. 13:10-15)—to cover up with empty talk. Worthless physicians, mere quacks, you are; with some mumbled incantations you think you can heal a person who is deathly ill. It would be better if you just kept your mouths shut; then at least we could apply to you the ancient proverb (Prov. 17:28): "Even a fool who keeps silent is considered wise." Before being able to act as a defender in a lawsuit, one must first listen carefully to what the accuser—in this case, I—brings up as grievances against the accused. So begin by considering seriously, with me, what it is that drives me to speak up publicly against God. I have a good many things against God; please do not immediately protest the fact that I am entering the lists against him, but start by realizing that for me this is an utterly serious matter. And if afterward you want to speak, then do not obscure the fact that I am in actual reality suffering unjustly, and do not use lies in your defense of God. It is simply a lie to say that all suffering is deserved punishment. If you really want to apply that false thesis to my case, you will first have to prove that I have committed sins that warrrant my misery.

But do you really think that God will take it if people choose his side, not because he is right, but solely because, after all, he is the mightiest? He who himself has said that he is impartial (Deut. 10:17) and very sternly forbids earthly judges to look at the person instead of the issue (Lev. 19:15)—would he be served by your partiality? The idea that God needs defenders, like yourselves at that, is ridiculous. Worse yet: he will react to it in high dudgeon, for he will, at a glance, see through your empty arguments and will know how to get you for it. One cannot falsely paint a pretty picture of appearances for him, as it sometimes works successfully among men. You will find out that he does not take kindly to any partiality, however subtle and concealed, even if it be partiality in his favor. Do not forget that it is *God* you are dealing with: the supreme Majesty, at whose voice of thunder human beings fall to the ground in panic. The quasi-defense you bring forward will not hold up, like an inscription carved in stone, but will blow away under pressure from the gentlest breeze, like words written in sand. The structure of your thoughts is a structure of clay—at the first real rainshower it will leak.

13:13-19 RATHER LISTEN TO WHAT I HAVE TO SAY TO GOD

I am going to risk it: I will direct my accusations against God, fully conscious of his power and majesty, and if I perish, I perish. I know that by opposing God I am risking my life— or what is left of it. I am like a man who does not hide his life inside his body but who takes it between his teeth or in his hands, so to speak; in a flash it can be taken away from him. If God in his anger over my boldness were to take away my life, it is all the same to me; I do not expect any good things to happen to me anymore anyway. I only want *one* thing: to talk through the issue between him and me and prove to him that my behavior does not deserve such treatment. And so I am venturing into his presence; and it might turn out to be liberating for me to lodge my protest against him face-to-face, for a godless man would never succeed in such a venture; he would not even be admitted into his presence. My very appearance before him, whatever the outcome be, would by itself be proof of my innocence.

So please listen—I am asking you again—with attention and openness to what I want to say to God. I have carefully prepared my presentation and am convinced that I am right. If anyone can refute me by offering solid proofs of evidence, then I will submit. Then I will not say another word and will accept death as the judgment I have deserved. But not before!

13:20-28 AT LEAST IF GOD IS PREPARED TO RESPOND IN REASON

If God is the one who can refute me, then let him do it. But then let it be in the form of a rational conversation. I am not now talking to my so-called friends anymore but only to you, God. I am appearing before you with my protest, but in order to have a rational conversation with you, two things are needed. You must stop beating me down; how can I speak to you and listen to you when you keep pouncing on me? And you must not overpower me with that mighty majesty of yours either; just let us face each other like two honest people. If you have something against me, then please follow the usual procedure: summon me to a trial, give your reasons, and I will respond with my arguments. Or if you wish to leave the initiative to me, then I shall be first to state my case and you may respond. Give me a summary of the debts and crimes you hold against me; just tell me what I, probably without knowing about it, have done against you. Why do you turn your face away from me as if you are my enemy? You do not imagine, do you, that I want to do anything hostile against you and do you harm? What would I be able to do to you, the Almighty? What am I, a mere harmless mortal, other than a half-dried leaf torn by the wind from its branch, or a dead blade of grass chased by the wind? There is no reason to be afraid of such a person, is there? Still, as a judge who submits written verdicts, you have brought bitter misery upon me and held me responsible for what I did before I reached the age of responsibility. In my thirteenth year I became a "bar mitzvah," responsible for my own actions. That was the beginning of a new life; but you would make me inherit the insolvent estate of my early years without benefit of an inventory. For you to thrust me into debt-slavery, tying me down with a ball and chain as though I were a criminal who would otherwise escape, is a violation of law. You will not let me go my own way even for a moment and have tattooed the soles of my feet as proof that I am your indentured slave. I, a human being at the point of death, fragile as a piece of rotting wood, about to disintegrate like a moth-eaten old coat—surely I am no threat to you?

14:1-12 A PERSON ONLY LIVES ONCE, AND THAT ONLY FOR A SHORT TIME

We human beings are not like you—without beginning or end, living from eternity to eternity. Our beginning was at birth; we are brought forth by a representative of the weaker sex and carry this weakness with us. It is not long before the process of becoming old and infirm begins, a process that is accelerated by the appearance of unpleasant surprises and new tasks. "He flourishes like a flower of the field," as one of the psalms (103:15) has it. The shadow of a tiny cloud flits across the plain and disappears: that is the life of a man. There is no real reason, is there, for you to initiate a court case against me as though I stood in your way? Of course you can point out shortcomings in every human being, especially when it comes to noncompliance with rules of ritual. That is how we are; no one is free from faults. But that does not hurt you, does it?

If you then have set such narrow limits to human life, limits that no man can transgress either by violence or by craftiness, then you need not worry, do you, as though he threatened your rule? Suppose he could injure you, still it is only for a moment and then he is gone. It is really not necessary to keep him under constant scrutiny. Really, every now and then you can leave him to himself, just as a hired laborer can also enjoy his leisure at the end of a workday.

Trees are different; if they are cut down, the following spring new shoots come up from the roots. Even if the roots appear to be dead, and the stump has rotted, rain only needs to fall to renew it, and to produce young life like that of a freshly planted sapling. Man is not so fortunate: all his vitality expires at death. Human beings are like the water in limestone country; somewhere in the depths some of the limestone dissolves and the water runs away in a subterranean channel. What was a lake becomes a plain; a creek becomes a dry bed. The water does not return. So a human being, once dead, does not rise to a new life. The heavens remain above the earth but for him there is no waking from the sleep of death. As long as the heavens remain—hence forever—a human being, once expired, remains in the clutches of death.

14:13-22 GOD DOES NOT GIVE A PERSON A SECOND CHANCE

How different it would be if after a period of death we could live again! I would have no grievance if you were to put me away for awhile in the realm of the dead, the way one hides a precious possession in the earth. If you hate me so, then let me put in time in the realm of the dead till my sentence is finished. But that is precisely the thing that does not happen; if that were the case, I could at least look forward to the end of my term of forced labor that you have imposed on me, till someone else could take over my job and I, after a period of rest in the realm of the dead, could begin to live again. Your voice would sound in the darkness and call my name; gladly would I answer: "Here am I!" and, not without some embarrassment over your long period of anger, you, too, would long to see me back again as part of your handiwork.

But now it is different: there will be no second chance. During this short unique life of mine you record every possible misstep. You do not immediately begin to punish; but with icy calm you put away into your portfolio as new proof of guilt the record of every transgression I might commit; you seal it and file it away, in order when the time comes to bring it up again and to exact your pound of flesh.

Your mills grind slowly—so that for a long time we think we are doing fine—but they grind exceedingly fine. The process is slow but irreversible, like mountains that erode under the wind causing rocks to lose their base of support and crash down, or like stones in a wadi that slowly wear down and the loose dirt is washed away. Slowly but surely our hope erodes. In the end you overpower a person by means of an incurable disease and he wastes away—his fresh and well-filled face, the product of his prosperity, becomes pale and thin, so that his friends no longer recognize him—just as my friends no longer recognized me when they came to visit (2:12). You leave him to his fate like a castaway wife or a useless slave. Then he languishes without interest in his surroundings, even when it concerns his closest family. He is aware only of the stabs of pain that cut through his body and of the powerlessness of his nearly expired self.

SECOND DISCOURSE OF ELIPHAZ 15:1-35

The gloves are coming off. In his second discourse Eliphaz no longer speaks of a better future, which Job, under certain conditions, might expect. What Job gets to hear is a torrent of attack and accusation. Now that Job is clearly not minded to take to heart the words of his friends, Eliphaz, in his impatience, becomes outright aggressive, plainly saying that Job may not regard himself as being without blame, and depicting at length the fate of the wicked, of whom—in the conviction of Eliphaz as he hints clearly—Job is one.

We can divide his discourse in four sections of somewhat varying lengths:

15:2-10   Job's arrogance toward men is intolerable.
15:11-16   Much more intolerable is Job's arrogance toward God.
15:17-24   It has been known of old: crime does not pay.
15:25-35   For every crime is a crime against God.

15:2-10 JOB'S ARROGANCE TOWARD MEN IS INTOLERABLE

You, Job, by your own words prove that you do not deserve the honorable title of wise man. Your opinions are windy; they lack substance and are unverifiable. They come forth from an interior that is inflated by thoughts as damaging as a sirocco, the east wind that scorches everything in its path. Your arguments hold no water; they are loose and unprofitable. In addition there is something very serious, Job: you cause the people to doubt the usefulness of a godly life. Before God a person has to choose his words with care, but you are a bad example to simple saints. The more strongly you express yourself, the clearer it becomes to us that behind your speech is a conscious or unconscious sense of guilt before God. An innocent man does not talk that way; only a person who tries craftily to cover up his sin uses such vehement language. The suspicion that one way or another you have sinned is not just my imagination. Your own words prove it. An innocent man does not need such verbiage. The longer you continue in this fashion, the more you will spoil your own case, for you will be condemned out of your own mouth.

When we hear you speak with such self-assurance, we would almost think that you are infinitely older and wiser than anyone else on earth, that your experience dates back to the beginning of creation (Ps. 90:2); in fact, that you were present when God met in council with his angels and decided to appoint human beings as administrators of the earthly creation (Gen. 1:26). True, if you had been present, then you would have been able to learn the deepest kind of wisdom: knowledge of God's own intentions for man and the world. But that is nonsense: your knowledge does not extend beyond ours. If experience is the best teacher, you have to acknowledge that what we say is the fruit of experience extending over more years than yours. What we have said so far contains the distilled experience of many generations; it goes back further than your knowledge or than what you may have learned from your father.

15:11-16 MUCH MORE INTOLERABLE IS JOB'S ARROGANCE TOWARD GOD

Our words of consolation were inspired by God; contradict us and you contradict God. Do you have at your disposal a deeper wisdom than that which we offered you in the name of God—a verdict hidden from all other people? By no means! You are carried away with your own very limited understanding and you act as if you can refer to something so powerful that you can turn your spirit loose against God and say what you please without paying attention to what we have confronted you with in the name of God.

You, a mortal, born like any other man of a woman, want to act as if God could not censure you for anything and as if you could rightly rebuke God for something. Not even the holy angels venture to do that; they have neither power nor wisdom outside of God. Not even the inhabitants of heaven can claim innocence before him, supposing now that they would dare to argue with him. Then what does a mere human being want? What do you, Job, want, you who have been clearly marked by your illness as one rejected by God, while from your words it is evident how sour and loathsome you are, like milk that has stood around too long. Unfairness toward God and man is all too congenial to you—you gulp it down with great eagerness as though it were a drink of cool water on a hot day.

15:17-24 IT HAS BEEN KNOWN OF OLD: CRIME DOES NOT PAY

Now listen carefully once to what I have seen in life. Not that it is only my observation; all really wise people know it and have learned it from their ancestors. And they were not just anybody; from ancient times Teman and all of Edom were famous for their traditions of wisdom (cf. Jer. 49:7; Obad. 8), which come down from a time when its inhabitants could live on the land assigned to them in undisturbed peace, before strangers frightened them with their raids. Well now; they learned that a transgressor of divine and human laws lives in perpetual fear, and shrinks at the thought of what is to come. Such a man knows no peace of mind; over and over it is as if he hears in his ears the trumpet signal indicating the approach of enemy bands. Externally he may perhaps prosper for a time, but he is afraid all the while that vengeance, coming in the form of ruthless bandits, will strike him. He hides in the darkness of his most interior room (cf. 1 Kings 22:25) and dares not come out again. He continually feels he is being spied on by powers that wish to deliver him to the sword.

When he—driven by his fears—wanders about in the desert, the vultures wheel in the air above his head waiting to devour him when he sinks exhausted and helpless to the ground. He knows this will happen to him; for he has brought this fate on himself by his own misdeeds. He is being readied for the day of darkness, a day of vengeance, and at the thought of it he is filled with horror, feels completely enclosed and unable to defend himself as though a king were marching his army against him. Such inner unrest is the inevitable consequence of unjustly acquired riches.

15:25-35 FOR EVERY CRIME IS A CRIME AGAINST GOD

Perhaps he thought that he was only hurting little people, people from whom he had nothing to fear. But anyone who violates either the person or the property of another is raising his arm, knowingly or unknowingly, against God the Almighty. In a mad dash to enrich himself he is storming at his victims with his neck outstretched in order to thrust them down to the earth. Or, if it concerned a larger number of opponents, he gathered a band of his subordinates who then charged at their defenseless prey with thickly bossed shields. He did not realize that in doing this he was attacking God Almighty, incurring a debt in his books. It simply did not occur to him, as a fat, contented man of wealth with heavy jowls and overhanging paunch, that he was doing this. Even cities that had been struck by a curse, as Jericho was at one time (Josh. 6:26), were welcome to him and he settled in them, together with his men, without giving a second thought to God's curse (cf. 1 Kings 16:34). He fancied he was only dealing with human beings and only cared about his own profit.

But that profit is a mere illusion. I see him as a vine planted on land where it cannot strike root. There is no real vitality in it; the grapes remain little berries that dry up so that their weight does not make the branches bend toward the ground. Its young shoots will shrivel in the summer heat, and when in the autumn the east wind begins to blow—the hot breath of God's anger—then its branches are torn away. Let him not think that he can save anything by craftiness or deception; his fellowmen treat him the same way. Evil boomerangs; the deceiver is deceived.

To return to the figure of the vine: its branches are cut off, not when it is time to prune, but when it is still budding, so that it cannot form any green foliage. Such an ill-fated vine loses its unripe fruit prematurely. Or consider the olive tree: it blossoms every year but bears fruit only every other year; in the off-years the blossoms fall uselessly to the ground. The man who injures his neighbor and so insults God is like the olive tree in the off-year. He and those who are like him never achieve anything permanent. Riches, gained through crookedness, are consumed in the fire of God. God knows the plan such scoundrels make: they are always devising mischief for their neighbors and to that end employ injustice and deception.

JOB'S REPLY TO THE SECOND DISCOURSE OF ELIPHAZ 16:1–17:16

Job's replies gradually get shorter. Eliphaz, by using aggressive language, provokes Job into answers equally aggressive. In just a few places (16:7; 17:2-4) he still addresses God; but when he does he appeals from God to God in a way that is puzzling to his friends and perhaps also to us. Here and there this excitement makes his argumentation—if we may still describe it as such—hard to follow, not only for us, but also for the ancient copyists of the Hebrew text and for the translators of antiquity. Our translation sticks as much as possible to the text that has been handed down but deviates from it in a few places (16:6, 20; 17:15-16). The sections, in which we have divided this reply of Job, are very unequal in length:

16:2-6	What use is comfort that is restricted to words?
16:7-14	It were better to realize what God has done to me.
16:15-22	Nevertheless, I will continue my appeal to God.
17:1-10	I have to do this, for among men I only encounter scorn.
17:11-16	Their talk about a better future makes no sense in my case.

16:2-6 WHAT USE IS COMFORT THAT IS RESTRICTED TO WORDS?

All that you assert has long been familiar to me. You apply the ancient traditions of wisdom to my case, but what you offer are generalizations that do not fit my condition and only have the effect of depressing me more. To you it seems to be well established that my own sins have caused my misery and so your so-called comfort only increases my trouble and grief. In my situation your wisdom is meaningless and I do not understand, Eliphaz, that you have the nerve to come back to me with such cheap talk.

Really, it is not difficult: if the tables were turned and you were mourning and sick, I could tell the same shallow tale. My, what a long speech I could offer, one that was full of ordinary talk about human sin and God's righteousness! I could wag my head over you, as you do now, in ready-made sympathy and not without looking down on you deep in my heart and with some secret inner pleasure. I would encourage you with words, only with words. You would have to be content with words—and experience no relief. And if I were silent, that would not help either; from me you would get no benefit whatsoever.

16:7-14 IT WERE BETTER TO REALIZE WHAT GOD HAS DONE TO ME

Now, however, the case is that I am in difficulties and you are on easy street. God has broken me. Besides—you, O God, by plunging me into mourning and misfortune, you have so terrified my whole community that everyone avoids me (cf. 42:11). Where are my brothers and sisters, where is the rest of my family, where are my acquaintances? They are afraid that my nearness to them will bring them misfortune, too. I sit here as a witness to misfortune and as a prime example of it; by looking at me people can tell what God can do to a person. To all of them my sickness is proof of my supposed sins, evidence that accuses me of evil I have allegedly committed.

Like a predator God has attacked me; time after time he has struck out at me. I can hear him gnash his teeth in anger and his eyes are filled with sharp condemnation. And that is not all: all people take God's side and turn against me. They shriek that I am an accursed sinner; I feel their scorn like blows to the jaw, and am in their midst as one against many. God has delivered me, helpless, into the hands of ruthless scum.

It is only a short while ago that all seemed to be well with me but of a sudden he seized me by the scruff of the neck, the way a lion seizes a kid, shaking it until the neck breaks. Let me choose another image: he practices his archery with me as target. The arrows fly all about me but often they strike home, piercing my most precious organs. Or to take still another figure: I am a besieged castle; one breach after another is made in my walls. Soon he will make the definitive attack on me and then I am finished.

16:15-22 NEVERTHELESS, I WILL CONTINUE MY APPEAL TO GOD

Another person might wrap sackcloth, as the garment of mourning, around himself for a little while; I have sewn my body into it as the one garment that always suits me. Like a wounded buffalo that crashes with its horns into the dirt, so I have been deprived of all my strength. I have cried so much my eyelids are red and my eyes dull. All this suffering comes over me, although I cannot imagine what I have done to deserve it. I have not enriched myself at the expense of my neighbors; in my prayers I have never asked for anything not due to me, let alone that I spread out hands full of blood to God in prayer, the sin of which Isaiah accused his contemporaries (Isa. 1:15) or Jeremiah the worshipers at the temple in his day (Jer. 7:9-10).

For that reason I also wish that the earth will not cover my blood when I die: I do not want my protest against the unjust treatment I have endured to be silent after my death. Let my blood speak even though I am dead, as Abel's blood cried out to God from the ground after his death (Gen. 4:10). But even now while I am still—do not ask me how—in the land of the living, I know that in heaven there are those who can testify to the injustice done to me by heaven. The same God who attacked me as though he were a wild animal, who as an archer used me for his target, and who stormed at me like a hostile army—that same God I call as witness for the defense, who can confirm my oath of innocence and act for me as friend and attorney. My tears constitute an appeal to him to enter into judgment with himself. Just as an earthly judge pronounces a verdict in the case that a plaintiff has brought before the court against the one who has violated his rights, so I expect that God will make the pronouncement that he has unjustly let all this misery come over me. And I want that to happen now, while I am still alive, for a human being has but a few years, I in particular. Once I have gone to that unknown land from which no traveler ever came back, it will be too late to act. God had better remember that: *he* may have plenty of time, *I* do not!

17:1-10 I HAVE TO DO THIS, FOR AMONG MEN I ONLY ENCOUNTER SCORN

I spoke of years just now, but I am all but dead now. I have no spirit left; I cannot do anything. My life is like a fire that has gone out; there is only a faint glow left in the coals. All this world can still offer me is the choice of a grave. Therefore I again come back to you, O God. You know that I am speaking in uprightness, and not loosely in scorn, and that the murmurings of my eyes—pardon the mixing of metaphors—that the complaint, which speaks from my dull eyes, does not arise from the recalcitrancy that utters mockeries. But, then, be my advocate! From your boundless reserves of compassion take out a security bond in my favor. I need not expect that people will pay my bail for me; you alone are left. Human beings have no insight in the perplexing fate that has befallen me; and so you do not grant them the honor of speaking on my behalf—however innocent I am. You will not elevate them to so high a position. They only seek their own advantage; they will inform on their friend for a share of the fine he will have to pay. You know it and punish the evil by striking at his family.

From the fate God has decreed for me they draw only one conclusion: this man Job must be a deeply fallen man. With them it has become proverbial: a sinner "like Job," a man who committed evil in secret but was disgraced by God at last. Anyone hearing my name will spit on the ground as a sign that he wants nothing to do with me. You may ask: "Do you really care what people think of you?" and I answer: "Yes, I care"; it is an additional source of pain on top of all my other suffering, and I pine away; my body is all gaunt and thin as a shadow when night falls. The fact that I give expression to my despair may disturb those fine upstanding citizens; it may offend people who have never, like myself, been indicted by the circumstances of their life, and who now make me out to be a God-forsaken hypocrite. Listen to their complacent talk: "An innocent person does not get upset when misfortune strikes. It is precisely at such times, in fact, that he proves his mettle!" That is how all three of you think, right? People like you can always, if you wish, fall back on talk of this kind, but you will not convince me. Your contempt proves that you have no insight into the exceptional nature of my case.

So I make my appeal to God and not to man.

17:11-16 THEIR TALK ABOUT A BETTER FUTURE MAKES NO SENSE IN MY CASE

My life is over, my illusions are ripped to shreds, my dreams frustrated. And now I have to listen to folks who want to encourage me with talk that says the darkest hour comes just before the dawn. Because it is pitch-dark around me I have to believe that the new day has almost dawned for me. I would have to hope that change for me is imminent, but in fact, for all practical purposes I have already entered the realm of the dead—I am pretty well established there. Like a child that has left his own family and been adopted in another, so now I have an adoptive father—the grave—and I have to accept those who live in my father's house—worms and maggots—as my mother and sisters. Why, then, do you speak of hope for me? Why stare into the future to look for happiness that is imminent for me? Will hope and happiness stay with me as I sink away to the realm of the dead? Is the process of dying not the most awful and absolute loneliness?

SECOND DISCOURSE OF BILDAD 18:1-21

It is striking that Bildad, in his second discourse, mentions God only once, and this in the last sentence, one which he, for that matter, puts into the mouth of future generations (v. 21). His speech really concerns the imminent course of the world as he sees it, more than God's action in it. He is past the point where he could still speak of a favorable turn of events that God could bring about in Job's lot under certain conditions. He proclaims but one theme: judgment upon the wicked (read: Job).

It is difficult to divide this judgment speech into approximately equal sections. An effort to that end may be found in the following arrangement:

18:2-4   You overestimate yourself at our expense.
18:5-10   I repeat: the wicked man comes to no good.
18:11-15   A miserable death awaits him.
18:16-21   Even his progeny will vanish.

18:2-4 YOU OVERESTIMATE YOURSELF AT OUR EXPENSE

In order not to get too personal I will use the plural "you" a few times, for there are more attackers of the wisdom handed down to us who talk just like you, Job, but it is you I mean. You waste our time with such talk. A real conversation is possible only if you return to the ancient, generally accepted insights. Of those insights we are the spokesmen and you ought to respect us for it. But you pay no attention to our words; you think yourself so much wiser than we and regard us as dull-witted as cattle. By doing this you make your situation even worse than it is. You are not prepared to adapt yourself to the world as it is; for your sake everything would have to be turned upside down, the cultivated field be made a desert, and rocks be dislodged from their place. But the world remains what it is: good earth remains good earth and a stone wilderness remains just that.

18:5-10 I REPEAT: THE WICKED MAN COMES TO NO GOOD

You may say (12:6) that the tents of marauders are safe and that those who provoke God are secure, but *I* say: The lights of the wicked are soon snuffed out and his little fire soon stops burning. Soon it grows dark in his life; and he has to stand helplessly by while his lamp goes out. A little while ago we saw him purposefully pursue his schemes but all of a sudden it is as if his feet have been caught in a trap. He cannot continue on the path on which he was traveling, his plans fail, and his intrigues ruin him. It goes with him as with a gazelle, for which the hunter has spread his net: the more swiftly the animal runs, the more surely it is caught; or as with a wild animal that does not know that the hunter has dug a pit on its accustomed trail and has covered it with a thin layer of plaited branches. Or the hunter sits hidden in the shrubbery, holding in his hand the rope that causes the trap to clamp shut, so that the animal is caught. The evil man is like an animal that inevitably gets caught in the snares hidden in the loose sand on the way to the water hole or in the trap set up for it.

18:11-15 A MISERABLE DEATH AWAITS HIM

As our friend Eliphaz has already said (15:20), the scoundrel is beset by terror all his life long. Terrors keep startling him and rob him of his rest. He is driven by fear, dogged by misfortune. It pursues him like a hungry predator; catastrophe always stands ready, like a huge rock over which he will stumble and fall. Death's first-born son, the disease that has attacked you, first consumes the ends of his fingers and toes so that they drop off, and then spreads to his hands, feet, arms, and legs. At last he has to leave this life in which he fancied himself secure and is confronted by the final horror: death. No son, no heir, or anybody else dares to take up residence in the house of a leper; it is left to rot, and God rains down sulphur upon it, as he did on Sodom and Gomorrah.

18:16-21 EVEN HIS PROGENY WILL VANISH

In all this he does not even have the satisfaction of knowing that his descendants will profit by his unjustly acquired possessions. He is like a dying tree: in root and branch he dies away and nothing remains of him, neither child nor progeny (cf. Isa. 56:3). Nowhere is there left a piece of land called "the field belonging to Mr. Rogue." For him there is no place left in the light of the land of the living, no place anywhere on the crust of the earth. In the tribe to which he belonged no descendant of his can be found any longer, and if he established himself under the protection of another tribe, even there there is no progeny to keep his name alive.

A hideous example—that is all he leaves behind. The younger generation takes note of it with a shudder, and the older generation, his contemporaries who knew him in the days of his pride and power, get goosebumps as they come past the ruin of his house and other buildings. Then a father, in warning, will say to his sons: "This house and this yard belonged to someone who sought—in violation of God's commandments—to hurt his fellowmen."

JOB'S REPLY TO BILDAD'S SECOND DISCOURSE 19:1-29

Job answers Bildad's rebukes and words of judgment with vehement accusations directed toward his friends. Now that he has found no solace in their company, there remains for him no alternative but—notwithstanding all that God has done to him—again to make his appeal to that same God. Whereas in his reply to the second discourse of Eliphaz he still addressed God a few times, he speaks only to his friends now. He no longer addresses God, but he does testify to his certainty that in the end God will acknowledge that he has rightly protested against his lot. The words he uses (vv. 25-27) belong to the most difficult passages in the entire book and have been interpreted very divergently in the course of the centuries. Our elucidation tries to stick as closely as possible to the traditional text but deviates from the interpretation that Jewish scribes have given, as is evident from the vowel points they have added, to these puzzling verses. To follow the argument more easily one can divide this chapter into the following sections:

19:2-6	You do not have to torment me; God does it quite adequately.
19:7-12	God has disgraced me.
19:13-20	As a result I am estranged from everyone.
19:21-27b	But in the end God will vindicate me.
19:27c-29	Then your judgment will come.

19:2-6 YOU DO NOT HAVE TO TORMENT ME; GOD DOES IT QUITE ADEQUATELY

You, Bildad, started your second speech with the phrase "How long?" I am taking the phrase over: "How long"—do you plan to torment me? Instead of consoling me, you only increase my suffering by arguments designed to show that I myself am the cause of my suffering. By talking in this fashion you are busy crushing my spirit. Just as the patriarch Jacob in his impatience charged Laban that he had changed his wages ten times (Gen. 31:41), without actually calculating each case on his fingers, so I say now that you have already come down hard on me ten times to get me to confess a list of secret sins. Suppose for a moment that I have erred, that I have granted hospitality in my heart to some sin or other, so that you might really correct me from the heights of your virtue and could bring into the fray my humiliation in misfortune and sickness as an argument against my claims of innocence—I deny that I erred but suppose now I did err—then you would still have to admit that God has laid on me a worse punishment than I would have deserved. In any case, it is God who has cornered me; it is not fitting that you should kick me with an extra kick while I am down. God is not well served by that approach.

19:7-12 GOD HAS DISGRACED ME

I can cry bloody murder but it does not affect him. When threatened by an enemy on earth one can lodge a complaint with a judge, but there is no appealing against God. I just followed the path of my life but have now come upon a barricade that God erected on it. Darkness is all about me; I cannot go on and I see no way out. In the eyes of people—in yours, too—I am a condemned criminal, deprived of the signs of my dignity. He has ruined the house of my life and I am perishing. Like the life of an uprooted tree, all my expectations have withered. The pain of my fever is to me the heat of God's judgment, a judgment like that which he inflicts on his enemies, among whom he also counts me. He marshals illnesses as though they were his troops and marches them against me. As though I were a fortified city he lets them build ramps against my walls in order to carry up the battering rams. Actually, that is putting it much too grandly, for all I can be compared with is the tent of a nomad. That tent is surrounded on all sides; I cannot escape.

19:13-20 AS A RESULT I AM ESTRANGED FROM EVERYONE

None of my brothers, members of my tribe, have come to help me. They think: one so afflicted by God must be a great sinner, one with whom it is better not to consort. God might even turn against Job's helpers! My good acquaintances can think of only one thing to do: avoid me! That is safest for them! Ties of kinship or friendship are no longer valid; even strangers, people I allowed to live on my land as protégés, forget their duty to be grateful.

Even my female slaves think they are too good for me and no longer provide their services. My house-servant used to run when I beckoned him; now I literally have to beg him for help. My wife lets me know what an ordeal it is for her to come near me and my very own brothers, born of the same mother as I, find my odor repulsive. Little children have no respect for me; when I strain to rise to my feet, they run off. None of the men with whom I used to consult wants anything to do with me. I used to be bound to them with strong ties of friendship but when they see me now they take a walk around the block. So I sit here just by myself—skin and bones; my cheeks and lips are shrunken and my gums are bare.

19:21-27b BUT IN THE END GOD WILL VINDICATE ME

You, who have always been my friends, you could at least show me some pity. I have not brought this misery upon myself by my sins: it is God who has afflicted me with illness.

Why, then, do you want to add your blows to God's? Why do you gnaw away at my hopeless existence as false accusers? But if you do not wish to listen to me, then I want a later generation to know what has come over me. If only my complaint could be recorded as a formal objection against God and man, and that in some permanent form, as is done with extremely important matters; for instance, by means of an inscription on a thin sheet of copper, or as King Darius had it done at Behistun, by a word-for-word statement carved in stone with all the letter-grooves filled with lead, so that all later ages would be able to find out what an injustice has been done to me! But no—I do not need to make my appeal to some distant future generation. There is One who is fully acquainted with all this and him do I call my Champion and my Redeemer. Just as in human relationships it is the obligation of the nearest kinsman to buy the freedom of a member of the family who has fallen into slavery or, if that family member has been murdered, to avenge his blood, so I, too, though everyone has abandoned me, have a Champion and an Advocate. In the end he will intervene, in law, on my behalf, against people who by comparison with him are only dust and ashes (cf. Gen. 18:27). When he rises to speak in my trial, then all my opponents, including you, will be cut down like so much underbrush that hurts one's feet in the forest (Isa. 10:34), and I shall see him, my Messenger of joyful tidings, who will announce my acquittal as the supreme Majesty: God, the same God who now punishes and humiliates me. Other people need not notice it; for me it is enough if I myself will see him thus in action as my Champion.

19:27c-29 THEN YOUR JUDGMENT WILL COME

My heart shrinks within me when I notice what it is you are thinking and making me feel: "That Job is so paranoid, he thinks the trouble is everywhere but in himself; but the cause of his misfortune is only to be found in his secret misdeeds!" But beware! There is a rigorous law (Deut. 19:16-21) that says that, when it becomes evident that someone has falsely accused another, the punishment that was intended for the other, must then be imposed on the false accuser. The sword of the executioner is threatening you! A divine judgment awaits all slanderers!

SECOND DISCOURSE OF ZOPHAR 20:1-29

Generally speaking, Zophar's second discourse presents few difficulties; nor does it have much depth. He repeats again the things that have been said before any number of times by him and his friends, it being understood that, just as in Bildad's second discourse, the call to conversion and the prospect of a better future for Job are missing. Again, it is the theme of judgment over the man of unjustly acquired wealth—read: Job—that is struck throughout.

Any number of details in this chapter, however, confront the translator with often insurmountable difficulties. Our translation [underlying the paraphrase] differs at a number of places from the RSV but makes no claims, any more than the RSV, to finality.

We wish to divide this chapter as follows:

20:2-9   The joy of the scoundrel is of short duration.
20:10-19   His unjustly acquired possessions do not prosper.
20:20-29   Unrest awaits him now; a wretched death later.

20:2-9 THE JOY OF THE SCOUNDREL IS OF SHORT DURATION

Because of what you, Job, have just said to Bildad, I must repeat what I believe. I must vent the indignation that your words have stirred up in me. I feel personally insulted by what you have said to my friend. It is beyond me that you dare to speak to us like that. We represent the wisdom and the insight gained by the wise from their experience since humankind was put on earth (Gen. 2:15). All generations can testify that the joy of unrighteous men of wealth is only of short duration: it is a cry of evil pleasure that dies out in icy silence.

Such a scoundrel may fancy himself to be far above all human morality and divine laws but what he produces—to use a drastic image—is of no more value or permanence than his own excreta: it passes with a bad smell and his existence, so bound up with it, comes to an ignoble end. Those who looked up to him with admiration, fear, or resentment soon ask themselves: "Where is the great man of violence?" For all who knew him he was a nightmare, but like a nightmare he vanishes. No one sees him anymore; we remember where he lived but his place is empty.

20:10-19 HIS UNJUSTLY ACQUIRED POSSESSIONS DO NOT PROSPER

The victims of his injustice, the people whom he has reduced to beggary, now come to his heirs with rightful claims to the restitution of their property, and these, then, have to satisfy the claimants by returning that which has been taken from them by devious means. Perhaps this already happens before he is dead and he himself, however painful it is for him, will have to return his unjust gains to the lawful owners. His bones—his entire personality—are full of secret sins: his entire existence was focused on the ruination of his neighbor and with this burden of guilt on him he goes down to his grave.

It is true: he enjoyed his own cunning; he sucked on it as though it were candy that he kept under his tongue as a wonderful treat and he enjoyed as long as he could. He could not leave it alone; sometimes he held it to his palate till he had swallowed the last trace of sweetness. But then what happens? "It is not good to eat much honey," as an ancient proverb says (Prov. 25:27), and that is his experience: his stomach rebels and the sin, which tasted so good, turns into poison in his belly. That which seemed to be sweet turns out to be bitter as gall—like snake poison. All he had gained by crooked means he now has to throw up, like someone who has eaten too much heavy food. God works in this process; he takes care that his stomach, that old glutton, is emptied in disgrace; all his riches go down the drain. And not only that! The possessions he has stolen poison him and bring him to a miserable death, as though a snake had bitten him and squirted his venom into him.

He must not think, therefore, that his prosperity will last. It may seem as if he were living in a lotus-land where the rivers brought him honey instead of water and the brooks carried fluid butter, but he will have to surrender all he has acquired with so much trouble. He cannot swallow, or digest, all those riches. He is rich enough to buy the things he wants, but he cannot enjoy them for any length of time. For they are unlawful gains: he loaned money or seed-grain to those who had gotten into difficulties; he demanded it back with high interest, and if they could not pay, he took possession of their field or home, without caring what happened to them afterward. But there will be no time for him to rebuild the house he took by force.

20:20-29 UNREST AWAITS HIM NOW; A WRETCHED DEATH LATER

He always wanted to increase his possessions, by whatever inhuman means, but when God's judgment comes over him, all his treasures cannot save him (cf. Ps. 49:6-10). He would not let himself be restrained either by rules of decency or by feelings of compassion; for that reason God will see to it that his prosperity is broken down. Of course, he knows that, too, governed as he is by the fear of losing anything or of missing out on some little advantage. That fear is realized, worse than he could suspect: one misfortune after another batters him. The fire of God's wrath breaks out over his devious practices; his fat man's belly will soon be distended with judgment and his skin tortured by the consequences of his sins, which come back on him like rain.

It will go with him as it is written by an ancient prophet (Amos 5:19): if he manages to escape one danger, another strikes him. Fleeing does not help; the enemy who threatened him with the sword shoots him in the back with a bronze-tipped arrow. When he pulls it out it proves to have pierced his gallbladder. In utter terror he expires.

Perhaps he had hidden stores of grain somewhere in his fields (Jer. 41:8). They will never come to light again. If years later they are discovered by accident, the grain will have turned black as though it had been burned, not by a fire kindled by men but by divine decree. That is how it will also go with the goods he had buried under the ground in his tent (cf. Josh. 7:21)—mold and corrosion, God's fire, will have made it worthless (cf. James 5:2-3).

Heaven and earth, angels and men, will rise against him as witnesses for the prosecution. A cloudburst causes the brook near his house to swell so high that its foundations are undermined; it collapses and becomes a palatial ruin (Luke 6:49). The day of God's wrath, a day of judgment for that man, will come over him like an irreversible flood. Just as our friend Eliphaz has said (18:21), so I will also say now, and it is my final statement: God has decided long ago to ruin and wipe him out. As the Supreme Judge he has reached his verdict and it will be carried out in God's good time. It has been pronounced over you, Job, and we see before our eyes that it is being carried out.

JOB'S REPLY TO ZOPHAR'S SECOND DISCOURSE 21:1-34

Job no longer addresses God now, any more than he did in his reply to Bildad's second discourse; he only speaks to his friends, particularly Zophar. His tone is so sharp that Zophar will not take part in the third cycle of dialogues. The common ground needed for discussion proves not to exist, and to Zophar's suggestion that Job has called down his misfortunes on his own head by a series of secret sins, Job replies with the accusation that the words of his friends, words meant to be consoling, only mean the betrayal of their long-standing friendship (v. 34).

We shall divide Job's reply as follows:

21:2-6	Please realize how utterly disconcerting my misfortune is.
21:7-26	Scoundrels live and die in prosperity.
21:17-26	God makes no distinction between the evil and the good, therefore.
21:27-34	Your arguments have no foundation.

21:2-6 PLEASE REALIZE HOW UTTERLY DISCONCERTING MY MISFORTUNE IS

As I did in my first reply to you, Zophar (13:17), I have to ask again for your compassionate attention to what I say, before you or the other two begin to present arguments that do not apply to my wretched lot. Believe me, if you would listen to my complaints seriously and with understanding, that would be more comforting to me than all you have said so far. Permit me to pour out my heart; after that you may reply—but I know ahead of time that what you will then have to say to me will sound in my ears as mere mockery.

I do not want to accuse you, or anybody else on earth; my complaint is directed to God. For that reason you need not feel insulted by what I say. In dialogue with human beings one has to observe the ceremonies and be considerate, but before God a man may freely express everything that is in his heart. He is not upset when some impatient word escapes our lips (cf. James 1:5). But even to men my impatience ought to be understandable; if you were really to take account of what has befallen me, you would be appalled and realize that no words would help here. You would be silent, just as you were silent for seven days after your arrival here (2:13). I myself do not know either how I am to interpret my fate: one's soul and body shudder at God's incomprehensible decrees.

21:7-16 SCOUNDRELS LIVE AND DIE IN PROSPERITY

You assert that the prosperity of the wicked is only of short duration (20:2-9), but I have observed that they attain a ripe old age and, despite their age, lose none of their power and influence. I have lost my children, but they see their children daily, and the children have by no means run away from their parental home, as Bildad said (18:9). They live on in the midst of their people and their families, and delight in their grand-children. Nor is it true that they live in perpetual fear as a moment ago (20:22) you, in imitation of Eliphaz (15:20-24), maintained. They do not feel anything of the disciplining rod of God—a subject you have harped on so often. Just note how well it goes in their enterprises or home life. The cattle may be owned by someone very wicked but the herds increase. They do not anxiously keep their growing sons at home; they allow them the free run of their lands, like sheep or goats that can find their own way, and their numerous children dance about when they play wedding. The parents have their feasts and sing to the tune of tambourines, stringed instruments, and flutes. So their days pass in the enjoyment of everything a person may want and, when the end comes, they pass away in rest and peace.

These, then, are people who do not care about God and want as little as possible to do with him. The language of their entire life was clear: they wanted no truck with a God who points to righteousness, faithfulness, and humility as the true path of life (cf. Mic. 6:8). According to their unexpressed opinion they did not have to serve the Almighty: by their own work—by their own sins against their neighbor, if you will— they had acquired everything they might need for a pleasurable life. Why should they knock on God's door by prayer? In their riches they had no need for God. Please understand: that is their—unexpressed—opinion; I myself know very well that their good fortune rests not on their own strength but on God's providence. Far be it from me to agree with such thoughts! But that is precisely the worst part for me: that God just permits them to do as they please and does not subject them to judgment.

21:17-26 GOD MAKES NO DISTINCTION BETWEEN THE EVIL AND THE GOOD, THEREFORE

As a really wise man has said (Eccles. 8:14): "There are righteous men to whom it happens according to the deeds of the wicked, and there are wicked men to whom it happens according to the deeds of the righteous." I would almost say that this is the general rule, for we seldom see that, as Bildad asserted (18:6), the lamp of scoundrels is suddenly snuffed out, that the ruin they have deserved really happens to them, and that God visits them with pain and illness in his wrath over their wicked lives. When in our daily experience do we see in actual operation the statement that the wicked are as chaff scattered by the wind (Ps. 1:4)? You may say, of course, that God wreaks his vengeance upon the children of the wicked (5:4), and this is also the plain message of the second commandment (Exod. 20:5), but it would be much better if the wicked man himself were punished in his lifetime. Let him experience his own downfall and drink the poison cup to which the supreme Judge has condemned him (Ps. 75:8; Jer. 25:15-29). For once a man is dead he is no longer affected one way or another by the fate of his descendants. Life is over; in the realm of the dead one has no knowledge of what happens to one's children or grandchildren.

Of course I know what you are thinking: here is Job who genuinely believes he can give God a lesson in how to run the world—that God, mind you, who not only rules our visible and temporal society, but is also the supreme Ruler over the spirits in heaven! I answer: there is not a trace of the law of retribution to be seen in this world. It is you who claim that God punishes evildoers, possibly after they die, in the lives of their children, but I see something totally different. I see people who literally swim in prosperity; they are never short of dairy products and even in old age they are not troubled by bone diseases or the like. At last they die, but in perfect peace, without any painful breakdown of their body, and without anxiety or fear. I also know of people who experience adversity throughout their lives, who never really enjoy themselves, and die in bitterness. Both the lucky and the unlucky ones are carried to their graves and there they lie in the dust, a prey to worms, sharing the same fate. Death is no compensation for those who had it bad in this life and no punishment for those who enjoyed themselves. With the Babylonian wise man I say: "Climb the ancient ruins and look around; consider the skulls of the earlier and the later ones. Which of them was an evildoer and which a benefactor?"

21:27-34 YOUR ARGUMENTS HAVE NO FOUNDATION

O, I know very well what you have in mind and have expressed with ever-increasing clarity: the misfortune that strikes a person is proof that he has sinned against God and men. By that attitude you do me a gross injustice. You say: "Nothing remains of all the possessions of the powerful who abused their position, or of the scoundrels who enriched themselves at the expense of the poor." Well, nothing remains of my riches—so, by your reasoning I must have been a mighty bad scoundrel.

Have you never consulted the travelers on the long road of life? You can ask them about the road they have taken, and request them, as they travel on, to give a fire signal after crossing a difficult pass or traversing a steep river valley—speaking plainly: you can consult people with a lot of experience concerning the sum of it all. They will tell you that they have found that it is precisely the wicked who survive catastrophes and who come safely through the day of judgment as though they were carried by angels.

Take such a greed-motivated man of wealth: who would venture to twit him for his way of operating and who will avenge the evil practices of which he is guilty? The truth is very different: everyone defers to him and shows him respect; and when for him the end comes, as it does for everyone, he gets a beauty of a funeral. They take him to a monumental tomb, which was hewn out of a rock during his lifetime, and fill the opening, through which he was brought to his final resting place, with dirt, so that his bones will not be disturbed by anyone. If he had any awareness of it all, people would say, "How comfortably he lies there!" Numerous people accompany him on his final journey, some walking ahead of the bier, others following behind it. Just where is the retribution?

In short: your reasonings concerning retribution—arguments with which you tried to comfort me in the beginning, but I now feel are unjust and a putdown—have no foundation in reality. I realize you are trying to refute me but I see in all those efforts nothing but a betrayal of our long-standing friendship.

THIRD DISCOURSE OF ELIPHAZ 22:1-30

In his final effort to bring Job around to other views Eliphaz now puts it very plainly: Job must be a very great sinner, or else all this misery would not have come over him. He lists a variety of concrete sins committed by Job, not so much against God but against God's creatures, particularly the poor and the powerless. It is not Eliphaz's intention to say that he himself has witnessed Job's antisocial behavior, but he does list a number of possible acts of injustice and unkindness with the idea that Job may recognize in some of them his own past deeds.

In distinction from Bildad and Zophar he continues to believe in the possibility of a better future for Job: if only Job will repent and, having removed his ill-gotten gains, turn again to God in humble prayer, when Job, too, will discover that God gives grace to the humble (1 Pet. 5:5; James 4:6).

We shall divide this chapter in three pericopes of nearly equal length:

22:2-11   Piety brings no entitlements, but sin is punished.
22:12-20   The high God brings about the downfall of the unrighteous man.
22:21-30   But if you repent of your greed, God will save you.

22:2-11 PIETY BRINGS NO ENTITLEMENTS, BUT SIN IS PUNISHED

You yourself have said, Job, that the things people do cannot injure God (7:20). The opposite is also true: the good deeds of a man do not profit God. God needs no man. If a person's conduct is irreproachable, as you claim yours to be, he has not by that token rendered to God any service that God would then have to reward. The meaning of a man's wise, that is, godly, behavior lies in the life of that man himself; piety is its own reward. It does not entitle him to compensation from without. If you do obey God's commandments you have done no more than your duty (cf. Luke 17:10). You must not think that by your blameless behavior toward God and man you are doing God a favor and can therefore count on a return favor.

But do you think by any chance that God opposes you on the basis of your good behavior and that he has gone into judgment with you for that reason? From the judgment that has befallen you we can infer only one thing: God has a long list of sins—too long to enumerate—to charge you with. Just let me mention a few things that rich people tend to do; perhaps you will recognize something of your own conduct here and there. Someone comes to make a small loan from you and you demand a pledge as security on the loan—something that is totally unnecessary for a wealthy man like you. You force him to give you his outer garment as a pledge, so that he has to go home in his underclothing. . . . A poor exhausted wanderer comes to your house but you begrudge him a cup of cool water; an emaciated and hungry man asks for charity but you deny him even a piece of dry bread. But when some man of power or influence comes to see you, you generously place all your land at his disposal; if you know that someone like that is the king's favorite, he can establish himself on your land, put up his tents and stay as long as he pleases. But poor widows are not welcome on your doorstep and you do not recognize the right of orphans to your protection.

So now you are caught in every direction in the mazes of the hunter's nets, as your friend Bildad so vividly pictured the lot of the rich scoundrel (18:8-10). You are too afraid to know what to do. In other words, a sudden darkness has come over you so that you cannot see a road clearly enough to go on it. Or, to use still another image: you are like someone walking through a dry wadi; all of a sudden water from a higher level comes roaring down and drags you along, powerless.

22:12-20 THE HIGH GOD BRINGS ABOUT THE DOWNFALL OF THE UNRIGHTEOUS MAN

God does not sit somewhere on the horizon, a place only a couple of hours distant, from which he can survey the scene. He is enthroned in the highest heavens, above the most distant stars, and from here he can oversee the whole universe, everything he has created. No man escapes his attention. Just as we sing of the sun (Ps. 19:6), "Nothing is hidden from its heat," so we can also say of God, "No one's sins escape the heat of his judgment." But it seems that you thought—with reference to your acts of injustice and unkindness—that God would not notice them, that his eyes could not penetrate the darkness of the night, or that the thunderclouds, which screen him from human eyes (Exod. 2:21; Ps. 97:2), would also keep him from seeing your behavior. Certainly, God lives in the heavens, but that does not mean that what happens on earth can escape his attention. Do you not know the psalm (113:5-6) that says: "Who is like the Lord our God, the One who sits enthroned on high, who stoops down to look on the heavens and the earth?" [NIV]. Thoughts like the ones you have evidently fostered are the thoughts of evildoers who say, "The Lord does not see; the God of Jacob does not perceive" (Ps. 94:7). But if you would follow their path, you will also have to share their fate. In the midst of life they are torn from their earthly existence. They have built their house on sand, and when the rains come down they carry away the foundations.

Where the mansion stood shining in the sun, a river now swirls. They did not want any dealings with God and were convinced that God could not touch them. The fools did not understand that all their prosperity was only due to God's patience. But I really do not want to spend any more time thinking about them; just like you (21:6) I say—and with much more justice: "I will never identify myself with the ideas of such people!" Only this yet: when such judgment comes over them, the poor who have been exploited by them can rejoice (Ps. 58:10) and laugh with scorn over the downfall of the exploiters. They themselves are destroyed and whatever they may have left behind is consumed by the fire of God's wrath.

22:21-30 BUT IF YOU REPENT OF YOUR GREED, GOD WILL SAVE YOU

Once more I will give you the only good advice there is: Do not oppose God, do not set yourself up against him, but continue to cultivate good relations with him. Then you will soon notice that your life will become smooth again. If you repent you will reap a harvest of rich blessings. To that end it is necessary above all that you let yourself be instructed by God: that is what it means to cultivate good relations with God. His commandments must govern your conduct. If you return to God then the ruins of your life will be built up again. But then you must, in the second place, remove from your house and possessions all the riches you have unjustly acquired. Do not, like Achan (Josh. 7:21-22), bury stolen treasures in the ground under your house or tent. It is better to scatter into the dust outside those pieces of gold ore that you accumulated; that fine gold of Ophir (1 Kings 9:28)—throw it between the rocks of the wadi. I mean, do not let the gold remain your idol. Has a prophet not said (Isa. 2:20) that when God comes in judgment men will throw to the rodents and bats their idols of silver and their idols of gold?

There is but one true treasure: intimate association with, and obedient service to, the Almighty. That is where true joy lies; on him your eye must ever be fixed with eager expectation. Then you will be able to pray to him with the assurance that he will hear your prayer, and you will soon, and with joy, carry out the vows you utter in your prayer in the event that he listens to you (Ps. 116:14). You need not fear that your good plans will fail. The darkness that now surrounds you will clear up, for "the path of the righteous is like the light of dawn which shines brighter and brighter until full day" (Prov. 4:18).

God wants nothing to do with people who are proud of their riches and power, but to the humble he shows favor (Prov. 3:34; cf. James 4:6; 1 Pet. 5:5). Humility above all means that you do not defile your hands with the blood and sweat of your fellowmen. If you take care that this is your case, you will escape the judgment that otherwise will fall inescapably upon you. This is my final word; it is now up to you!

JOB'S REPLY TO THE THIRD DISCOURSE OF ELIPHAZ 23:1–24:25

Job's voice comes through clearly in chapter 23 but in the course of chapter 24 we encounter difficult questions. This is particularly the case with 24:18-25, in which the point is made that the unrighteous man of power may temporarily succeed in his evil practices but that he will soon come to grief. Such observations fit far better in the discourses of the three friends, where this theme is struck endlessly, than in Job's mouth. We are forced to believe that in the transmission of the Book of Job something has gone wrong at this juncture. Bildad's discourse, 25:1-6, is exceptionally short; one would be disposed, therefore, to include 24:18-25 in Bildad's third discourse. It is not possible, however, to place the argument that the prosperity of the wicked is only of short duration right after 25:6; the transition would be too abrupt. It is still less likely to have come before 25:2; 24:25 is very obviously the conclusion of the entire speech.

Or is Job speaking again in this verse? But it does not fit well after 24:17 either, and the entire section, 24:13-27, concerning misdeeds committed in darkness, is hard to bring into any kind of relationship with the wretched lot of the oppressed. We would at least expect that the passage, if it does contain the words of Job, would end with the assertion that God does not, as a rule, punish the violations of the sixth, seventh, and eighth commandments depicted here (cf. the conclusion of 24:12).

We are inclined, therefore, to regard 24:25 as the conclusion of Job's reply to Eliphaz; this reply then embraces
23:2–24:12, plus verse 25. We should view 24:13-24 as an er-
ratic piece that has been moved from its original place, one
that we cannot determine. We can say only this much: we are
dealing here with words from one of the three friends, probably Bildad.

Adhering to the traditional form of the text we can divide
these two chapters as follows:

23:2-9	If only I could argue my case in a personal conversation with God!
23:10-17	Despite my innocence, his presence would disconcert me.
24:1-12	The fate of the dispossessed is wretched.
24:13-17	Evildoers do their work by night.
24:18-25	God's vengeance comes over unrighteous men of wealth.

23:2-9 IF ONLY I COULD ARGUE MY CASE IN A PERSONAL CONVERSATION WITH GOD!

You, Eliphaz, were so kind—unlike Bildad and Zophar—as
to consider a better future for me a possibility, and described
it with your usual eloquence (22:21-30). But I am not concerned with a possible future but with the present, and that
can only be called totally inexplicable misery. It is this that I
oppose in my complaint and indictment. Discouragement
causes me to let my hands hang heavily by the side of my
body: they are too heavy to raise in prayer, as you advised
(22:27).

For that matter, such a petition to God makes sense only
if he is prepared to be reached by one who prays, but this is
precisely where my distress lies; namely, in the fact that I
cannot find a way to God. I would love to appear before his
judgment seat; I have no doubt whatsoever that I have not
deserved this suffering. An earthly judge would certainly give
me the opportunity to defend my rights—rights that have
been violated. If only I had a chance quietly to explain my
case before the heavenly Judge! I have arguments in plenty.
I would also listen to what he would have to say in reply and
his verdict, I am sure, would be reasonable and comprehen-

sible. No earthly judge will try to overpower a plaintiff in his court; quite the contrary, his first duty is to be interested in the person presenting a complaint before him. May we not expect as much from the Judge in heaven? Does he not listen to the arguments of a person in distress? An honest man should surely be able to plead his case before the judgment seat of God and go home as a free man.

But where is that judgment seat and where is the heavenly Judge? I can look for him in all directions of the compass but I do not find him. He is a God who hides himself, both in his being and in his work.

23:10-17 DESPITE MY INNOCENCE, HIS PRESENCE WOULD DISCONCERT ME

I do not see God anywhere, but he sees me—he has seen me from my youth on—and he knows that I have always stuck to the right path. If he were to assay me, the way a goldsmith does with his materials, he would find my motives pure and unalloyed. The way he prescribes—the way of justice, kindness, and humility (cf. Mic. 6:8)—is the way I have always followed in my conduct toward God and men. What God has spoken by the mouths of his interpreters, the prophets, was always sacred to me and served as my guideline in my thoughts and action.

But God is unique. Gentiles see God as the head of an entire family of gods and goddesses, and so seek the intercession of members of that family, but I believe this is impossible. He has no wife or children who can restrain him when in his anger he goes too far. With him it is only his own will that matters. The things he has evidently decreed concerning me—the death of my children, the loss of my possessions, the hideous illness that ravages my body—all these things he has allowed to come over me, and, if he wants to, he can add new disasters to the list: it is all within his power. His will and his power know no limits.

Of course, I may from time to time express the wish to have a personal confrontation with him, but when I picture to myself what that would mean I know very well I would not be able or dare to say anything to him. His presence alone would completely overwhelm me and at the thought of him and me facing each other—he the eternal Almighty God, and

I a powerless mortal—I already shudder with fear. It is only the wish of a foolish man to have a personal meeting with God—but, still, it is from such an encounter alone that the solution of my distress could come. No one other than God has thrust me into this suffering. What has brought me to despair is not my dark fate by itself but the fact that God has brought all this upon me. Not loneliness, poverty, or illness is my problem but God's incomprehensible attitude toward me.

24:1-12 THE FATE OF THE DISPOSSESSED IS WRETCHED

In general I fail to see in the lives of people any trace of God's judgment upon the unrighteous and any sign of compassion with the victims of injustice and the underprivileged. Why does not God hold regular trials, so that people who, like myself, have ordered their lives in terms of intimate association with him can see with their own eyes that he is a God of justice and love?

Just look at how it goes among men! The rich grow ever richer—and with what means! They take possession of the patrimonies of others and move the boundary stones that mark off their property from the little fields of their poverty-stricken neighbors. Of course, they have their legal arguments for this purpose: those neighbors were deeply in debt to them. But it remains a cruel injustice to take away a person's means of livelihood. They do not even spare the flocks of sheep that the less-well-to-do could still permit to graze in community-owned pastures. Should a couple of fatherless children still own a donkey, it is led away to the stalls of the creditor to make up for an unpaid debt. A widow's only ox is taken away as pledge for seed-grain she has loaned—now how is she to plow her little field and sow that grain? The broad-shouldered man of capital defers to nobody; in the narrow streets of the village the poor have to stand back in door openings when he comes by.

In the morning when the wealthy landowners and their slaves leave their houses in order to work in the fields, the dispossessed also go out, not to the fields that have been taken from them, but to the uncultivated land around them, in hope of finding some odds and ends with which to still their hunger, as though they were wild donkeys that no one feeds.

Perhaps they find the remains of prey that hyenas and jackals have left behind—this, then, is food for their children. For the rest their "harvest" consists of wild herbs (cf. 2 Kings 4:39), which otherwise serve as mixed fodder for the cattle. It is a real treat for them if after the vintage they are allowed to glean remaining bunches of grapes (cf. Deut. 24:21). They no longer have the coat that would serve them at night as a blanket; they lack protection from the cold. When in the rainy season sudden showers come pouring down from across the mountains, they have no other protection than the sheer faces of the cliffs to which they cling.

Not even the children of the widow who has fallen into debt are safe from the clutches of the loan shark (cf. 2 Kings 4:1). These children are taken into slavery as pledges for unpaid debts (cf. Neh. 5:5). In harvest time these needy people who dress in tatters have a chance to earn some money, but they have to work all day before they get anything to eat, whereas a good landowner gives to his reapers a meal of parched grain after a couple of hours (Ruth 2:14) and God in his law takes care even of the threshing ox (Deut. 25:4). They roll heavy stone rollers over olives in a press but are not allowed to help themselves to the fruit of the olive trees. Hour after hour they tread out the juice from the grapes but not a drop goes to them to assuage their thirst.

So people perish of hunger and exhaustion; the groans of the dying are louder than the groaning of heavily burdened donkeys, and in death their souls cry out silently for help—but God remains unmoved; he seems to think all that social injustice is quite in order.

24:13-17 EVILDOERS DO THEIR WORK BY NIGHT

So much evil is done on earth! Some use the night, which was intended to give people rest, to indulge their evil lust. They seem to think that evil that is not seen by people can be done without risk of punishment. Let us follow, for a moment, the commandments of the second table of the law. Nightfall has come and the murderer gets up. He has no interest in hurting the rich; they have powerful friends and relatives who could avenge their deaths. It is the defenseless poor that constitute his prey; he prowls around like a thief to take the homeless by surprise from pure blood-lust. Night also serves as protection for the adulterer who in additon wraps a cloth around his face so that no one will recognize him. What is it to him that the seventh commandment says, "Thou shalt not commit adultery"? So also they dig holes through the clay walls of a house—perhaps only for the thrill of it—in order to break, unnoticed, into the storehouse and to fill a bag with grain. During the day they shut themselves in—as if behind sealed doors. They are enemies of the light—literally and figuratively. Other people gladly greet the light of day; these people welcome the deepest darkness of the night, which for them, familiar as they are with it, harbors no terrors. Their accustomed ways of acting are described in their own words in Proverbs 1:11-14.

24:18-25 GOD'S VENGEANCE COMES OVER UNRIGHTEOUS MEN OF WEALTH

Judgment, like a flood that washes him away, awaits the man who enriches himself by unjust means. People refer to his possessions as an example of how it will go with such a man: "May you lose your possessions as it happened with that man of capital!" He not only becomes poor; he gets sick, so that he can no longer stretch his legs in his beloved vineyards. Just as melted snow that fills the wadi in winter dries up in the course of the summer, so the unrighteous rich man fades away in death. The female slave, with whom he used to entertain himself more than with his lawful wife, soon forgets him as he becomes ill and dies. To her his body means no more than the maggots that cover it in the grave. A *crrrack!* and the dry piece of wood is broken: so it is with the rich man whose life is made up of unrighteousness.

That is how it should go with him; after all, what has he done in his life? He deprived a widow, who had no sons to protect her, of everything she had, leaving her stripped like an overgrazed field. Widows in general could not expect any good from him. He always succeeded, by the power of his wealth, in getting the rich and the powerful on his side. So— for a while he may be able to hold on, doing what he does, but then, unexpectedly, death will take him. He and his peers seem protected by their riches and on them they rely; but they do not realize that God, who is still patient with them, subjects all they do to close scrutiny. In their pride they elevate themselves above the ordinary man but all at once their game is over. Like weeds in the field, they have grown high, but collapse when the hot season comes, and are pulled out, root and branch, to serve as fodder for the cattle. Or, they stand high, like a field of wheat, but then the [grim] reaper comes and cuts off the heads of grain.

Upon the truth of all this I am prepared to swear an oath. How could anyone, who has kept his eyes open, refute what I have said? Who can prove it is not so?

BILDAD'S THIRD DISCOURSE 25:1-6

At this point we have to refer back to what we said in the introduction to 23:1–24:25, where we pointed out that Bildad's third discourse is exceptionally short, suggesting the possibility that 24:13-24 has drifted from its original moorings and was actually a part of Bildad's speech. There is nothing new in it; as it reads now, in this brief chapter, it is a repetition of what Eliphaz has already said in his first and second discourses. This is probably intentional on the part of the poet: the three friends, he suggests, have nothing more to say and can only repeat what has been said before.

25:2-6 BEFORE THE HIGH GOD NO MAN HAS ANY RIGHTS

Do you realize, Job, and are you sufficiently sensitive to, who and what that God is against whom you stir your audacious tongue? He is the omnipotent Ruler who by his mere existence inspires dread in all things that oppose him. Look at the starry heavens at night: God maintains unshakable order there; everything remains in place in this majestic procession. And can you number his troops, the stars in their constellations? And when God's light dawns over the horizon, who among the evildoers, who fancy themselves invisible at night (24:13-17), can call a halt to this ascending splendor?

It is as Eliphaz has already said in his first discourse (4:17): before God we cannot appeal to our supposed right. We are mere mortals, born of the weaker sex, the products of women. Even the moon is not all brightness but is full of spots, and I can only repeat what Eliphaz has said (15:15-16):

even the hosts of heaven, the angels and the stars, cannot claim to be pure in God's eyes—how much less, then, a man like you and us all, who by comparison with God are loathsome vermin that for a short while creep around on the crust of the earth!

JOB'S REPLY TO BILDAD'S THIRD DISCOURSE 26:1-14

The first three verses of Job's reply breathe a sarcastic spirit. The text then abruptly proceeds to describe God's omnipotence as it affects the shades in the underworld. The same power has manifested itself in the cosmic creation that is depicted in grand and, finally, mythological images. Job here approximates Bildad's glorification of God's omnipotence in 25:2-3, but whereas Bildad comes to the conclusion that man is too small to raise any questions concerning God's rule, Job concludes that man—the very same being—does not understand what God does. In short, Bildad recommends the acknowledgment of God's right; Job denies that man can arrive, in reason, at such acknowledgment.

This chapter divides naturally into two very unequal parts:

26:2-4   Must that be called "high wisdom"?
26:5-14   Who understands anything of God?

26:2-4 MUST THAT BE CALLED "HIGH WISDOM"?

Do you really think, Bildad, that you have in any way helped me with your statement? Here I sit in helpless misery; my feeble arms, thin as sticks, hang powerless by the side of my body—and you come at me with a glorification of God's omnipotence? Do you suppose that the silent recognition of human worthlessness before God produces any change in my personal suffering? Fine—I admit I do not, any more than anyone else, have the wisdom to fathom the enigmas of life, but your words contribute absolutely nothing to the clarification of my lot. You speak to me, claiming to be a messenger from God. Messengers are sent out, as a rule, by twos; who is your fellow-messenger? Messengers speak with the authority of

whoever sends them; whose thoughts are they that your words
transmit? God's? Go on—tell me another!

26:5-14 WHO UNDERSTANDS ANYTHING OF GOD?

When it comes to depicting God's omnipotence, Bildad, I believe I can do a better job than you. You mentioned God's
omnipotent government in the heights of heaven; but I know
that his omnipotence extends even to the abode of the dead.
The shades of the dead are there, in a place that is deeper
than any marine animal can dive, and they shrink at God's
approach when he deigns to show that the underworld also
is part of his domain. For in the realm of the dead, people are
not free, either, from his all-seeing gaze.

God's omnipotence? I know something of it, too. He
spreads out the high northern skies, with their circumpolar
celestial bodies that never dip below the horizon, as though
they were tentcloth. He it is who suspends this earth of ours
freely in space, supported by nothing. He packs the clouds
with rain like a bag that is too full, yet they do not tear. I
have been at the seacoast and seen the immeasurable circle of
the horizon, with its contrast between the light above and the
dark waters beneath, and I know that this, too, is God's
creation.

Every now and then his omnipotence is manifest in an
earthquake that causes the mountains—those pillars on which
the roof of heaven seems to rest—to shake and shudder, as
though they were alarmed by his overwhelming voice, the
thunder that accompanies an earthquake. Similarly, he demonstrated his power at the creation. The nations of the world
picture creation as having been preceded by a struggle of the
Creator against Chaos, conceived as a raging sea (Gen. 1:2)
that was stilled by him or as a monster, called Rahab, that
was defeated by him. When the original waters were brought
under control, the heavens extended themselves, like a lumi-
nous dome, above the earth (cf. Gen. 1:6-8). The defeated
power of Chaos was also called "Leviathan, the elusive ser-
pent" (cf. Isa. 27:1, and the old Canaanite conception pre-
served in a poem from Ugarit). I mentioned it also in my first
complaint (3:8). Whatever mythological representation of the
incomprehensible event of creation we may wish to use, this
is certain: by these means we only approximate the outermost

manifestations of God's activity as it concerns this world. They are but the least of the immense powers involved in it and even of these we observe but a few glimpses. Who, then, can claim to understand anything of the mighty word of creation by which God overcame "nothingness," the powers of the abyss (Ps. 33:6)?

JOB'S FINAL WORD TO HIS FRIENDS 27:1-23

In the first part of this chapter, 27:1-7, we again clearly hear the voice of Job who, notwithstanding everything God has done and his friends have said, clings to his conviction that he has not deserved the suffering inflicted on him. The second part, 27:8-12, also can very well be attributed to Job; a good argument for this thesis is the use of the second person plural in verses 11 and 12. The case is different, however, in the rest of the chapter. There we read that ill-gotten gains do not endure, an idea frequently expressed by the three friends (4:8-11; 5:2-5; 8:11-19; 15:29-35; 20:5-29) and rejected by Job (12:6; 21:7-21; 24:12). One must therefore assume that in 27:13-17 and 18-23 we are dealing with a fragment of the argumentation of the three friends belonging to the third cycle of the dialogues, perhaps originally a part of Zophar's missing third discourse. In any case it is remarkable that 27:13, the beginning of the passages we cannot possibly attribute to Job, is virtually identical with 20:29, the conclusion of Zophar's second discourse.

In accordance with the thoughts expressed above we shall divide this chapter in almost equal sections:

27:2-7   After all you have said, I still maintain I am right.

27:8-12   My appeal to God is proof of my innocence.

27:13-17   The wicked rich man cannot leave his children anything.

27:18-23   His house is blown away by a stormwind.

27:2-7 AFTER ALL YOU HAVE SAID, I STILL MAINTAIN I AM RIGHT

Swearing an oath by the living God, who punishes perjurers, I want again to declare my innocence against all your insinuations. I know very well that until now my protests have not moved him and that he has conducted himself like a judge setting aside a complaint as groundless, and that in fact he has, by his providences, thoroughly embittered my life—but perhaps a bit of perjury on my part might arouse him from his lethargy. If what I am about to say is not true, he had better let me die right here and now. For I am still alive—do not ask me how; the breath of life that God bestows for a time on man and beast (Ps. 104:29) is still present in me. I shall freely put it at risk when I declare under oath that all my protestations of innocence were and are true; not a word of mine was false.

For that reason I would not dream of granting that you are right or of pronouncing the confession of sin you demand of me. Far be that from me! As long as I am alive I will maintain that I am innocent. I am right when I say that I have not deserved this suffering as though I had committed some sin. When in my mind I retrace the days of my life I cannot find one of which I would have to say, on that day I dealt unjustly toward God or man. If people want to take that away from me, I only hope that God will unmask my opponents, namely you, who have deprived me of justice, as false accusers.

27:8-12 MY APPEAL TO GOD IS PROOF OF MY INNOCENCE

The fact that I can speak like this is proof that I have no sin to confess. A godless person would avoid such a confrontation with God. The Almighty would give him short shrift; his perjury would immediately evoke the death penalty. His appeal to the heavenly Judge would be immediately dismissed. It would only go badly with him if in his misfortune he were to look for redress from God. He would not get compensation, or even any kind of hearing, from God.

So from me and my wretched existence you can still learn something of God's power: if I had sworn falsely I would now fall dead to the ground. But I am still alive, although the Almighty could easily have let me die. That proves my oath is 100 percent true. You can see yourselves that after swearing that oath I am still alive—then why do you not want to believe my words, and why do you still cling to the illusion that I was plunged into this misery on account of my sins?

27:13-17 THE WICKED RICH MAN CANNOT LEAVE HIS CHILDREN ANYTHING

The men of great wealth increase their possessions by acts of injustice and violence—these too have an inheritance waiting for them at the hands of God, a legacy they deserve more than the property they have amassed: a violent death for their children and starvation for their descendants, all of whom expected a rich inheritance. If after war and famine there are still some survivors of the family left, they will perish in a plague, and will not be carried to the grave in the usual way, nor mourned by their widows, for the plague will have struck them all down and there is none left to pay the final respects to the dead. Their gravedigger will be the plague, which leaves their bodies at the place where the illness struck them down (for sword, famine, and plague, cf. Rev. 6:3-8).

What use is it for anyone to pile up bars and pieces of silver in his house, and to have more clothes woven and made than he or his dependents will ever wear? In the end, all this will be demanded by those whom he has injured in his life (cf. 20:10, 15); as it says in the Book of Proverbs (13:22), "a sinner's wealth is stored up for the righteous."

27:18-23 HIS HOUSE IS BLOWN AWAY BY A STORMWIND

A person like that, one who has piled up treasures for himself, can afford to have a palatial house built, but it is no more secure than a bird's nest that is torn down by wind and rain, or than the wretched little lean-to that the hired watchman in the vineyard has built for himself for protection against the heat. Soon a stormwind blows it down. The rich man lies down to sleep in his luxurious villa—but this is the last night he will spend in it. When he wakes up, a sudden gust of wind carries the roof off and away. Just as floodwater can rush down a dry riverbed like a wall of water, so a natural disaster startles the rich man out of his dreams of prosperity. A tornado from the eastern wilderness (cf. 1:19) pulled the roof off the walls by suction and carried it a short distance away; and the wall, which supported his bedstead, collapses in ruin. The explosive noises of a hurricane sound like the handclapping of a victorious tyrant; its whistling like mockery. The natural elements laugh in scorn at this seemingly well-built structure and its hapless inhabitant.

MAN UNDERSTANDS ALL THINGS, EXCEPT THE SECRET OF LIFE 28:1-28

As we observed in the Introduction (I.5), this chapter does not fit well between the preceding and the following chapters. The speaker is not so much Job as the poet himself. This hymn on wisdom is not addressed to the three friends, or to any one of them, or to God. It seems as if in this hymn the poet of the composition as a whole here draws his own conclusions from the futile efforts of Job and his friends to convince each other. It is very well possible that he had composed it at an earlier date and decided in the process of writing the larger work to insert it at this point. That could be an explanation for the fact that any reference or allusion to Job personally is missing, in contrast to the following three chapters in which Job is clearly the speaker. In its rich expressiveness and depth of thought the hymn is certainly not unworthy of the genius of the poet of the whole.

In terms of the structure of the content, taking note especially of the fact that verses 12 and 20 are practically identical, we can divide this chapter into three sections:

28:1-11   Man can worm through the earth in all directions.

28:12-19 But he cannot find the most precious thing there is: wisdom.

28:20-28 God alone understands it.

28:1-11 MAN CAN WORM THROUGH THE EARTH IN ALL DIRECTIONS

From the most ancient times man has searched the earth for precious metals and has been able to find them. There are places where silver can be found, and with a pan one can separate fine grains of alluvial gold from grains of sand. From banks of iron ore one can melt out iron, from copper ore, that yellow metal. But those are relatively simple procedures and it does not stop there. Men go down to the farthest recesses and uncover what has been hidden in the deepest darkness from when the world began by digging vertical shafts in the ground, and once they have come upon a layer of ore, they follow that layer, breaking through rock by way of horizontal shafts. When the shafts get deep the miners let themselves down by means of ropes and have no support for their feet. They dangle and sway in the air as though they were no longer human beings who walk on their feet.

The farmer, for whom the earth is a field in which after plowing the top layer he sows his grain, observes all this with alarm and estrangement. Mining radically ruins the land as though by a raging subterranean fire. Where mines have been dug and loose rocks and debris piled up around the pitheads, no crops can be sown anymore.

The mining industry can also focus on things other than metals: on precious stones enclosed within worthless rock. People break up everything to find sapphires—perhaps, although the word is not used, it is what we call *lapis lazuli*, which often shows goldlike dots, little "nuggets." The miners go down so deep that no animal will venture that far, no bird or creeping thing, and even the boldest of beasts, the lion, would not dare go down the shafts.

The men in the mining industry stop at nothing. However hard certain kinds of stone may be, much harder than the softer limestone that prevails in Palestine, like granite or basalt for instance, they know how to dig through and tunnel their way under the mountains. Here and there in the darkness of the shafts, lit up by little oil lamps, they see the precious stones shine or glitter. Neither are they daunted by subterranean veins of water; they follow them to the source and block them off. In the meantime they have discovered many precious substances that can now be brought to the surface.

28:12-19 BUT HE CANNOT FIND THE MOST PRECIOUS
THING THERE IS: WISDOM

In the mining industry, in addition to perseverance, much human intelligence also plays a role. But wisdom—knowledge of the factors that determine the lives of individuals and the destinies of nations—need not be sought among the "men of intelligence," the engineers. Then where must we look for it? People know where the layers of ore are located and follow them in their mining operations—but where is wisdom, that precious layer, embedded? No man arrives by himself at the secret of life. The Babylonians may claim that the god of wisdom dwells in watery depths, but however deeply the pearl divers dive into the sea at Elath, though they may find corals and oyster pearls, they do not find wisdom among them.

Nor can the merchant, who trades in silver and gold and travels to distant lands, find it anywhere for sale in the marketplace. He may have filled his coffers with gold from Ophir (southern Arabia or east Africa), which is considered very pure, or with even more precious stones, like chrysoprase (or dark-red carnelian) and *lapis lazuli* ("sapphire"; cf. v. 6); but he can exchange none of it for wisdom. Gold cannot be considered on a level with wisdom and the same is true of the elegant and precious objects that Phoenicians know how to make of glass. The work of the goldsmith gives to jewels of gold a value higher than the gold by itself is worth but in the pursuit of wisdom even the finest art object does not profit the merchant. The skillful craftsman can make things of great beauty from mother-of-pearl and mountain crystal, but they will not buy him wisdom. Not even the green chrysolite (or is it topaz?) that comes from the headlands of the Nile south of Egypt, which because it has to come such a distance and is so rare is more precious than gold, nor even the most refined gold, can compare with it.

28:20-28 GOD ALONE UNDERSTANDS IT

Where, then, can wisdom be found? And where is the insight that makes life with its many changes transparent? No mortal can tell and no birds, with their marvelous instincts, can point out the way to it. The Underworld and Death, viewed for a moment as powerful deities, have heard of it only by rumor (cf. 42:5); that is, at the outermost boundaries of human existence there is a suspicion that it must exist somewhere.

That is all a human being can say about it; man cannot go further than acknowledge his ignorance. Wisdom is God's secret. He surveys the entire scene and knows how to establish limits for the least tangible things: the force of the wind and the boundaries of the waters. In regulating the cosmic powers, rain and thunder, he fixed his eye on wisdom; he mastered it completely. He used it as an instrument with all of whose workings he was familiar (cf. Prov. 8:22-31). To mortals he did not reveal what, at its innermost, holds the world together, but limited them to the concerns of "practical reason": reverent obedience to the divine commandments and a life that shuns evil against God and men.

JOB RECALLS HIS FORMER DAYS OF PROSPERITY AND HONOR 29:1-25

After a short introductory sentence, which is identical with the first verse of chapter 27, we hear from Job in his own words how happy and respected he was in his earlier days. It is the counterpart to the prose description we read in 1:1-5. He enjoyed God's protection, as the Adversary pointed out in 1:10, was surrounded by his children, and was first among his equals, particularly because he always championed the cause of the disenfranchised. At the deliberations in the councils of the leaders his voice was decisive.

This description serves to bring out more vividly the contrast with Job's present state. The following chapter should really be taken together with the present one, therefore, but chapter 31 refers back to the past again, while in the same chapter the self-imprecations of Job relate to the future. Although the three chapters together constitute the grand concluding discourse of Job, we shall, for the sake of clarity, treat each of them separately.

We shall divide the first in four pericopes:

29:2-6	How happy I was under God's protection!
29:7-11	Everyone showed me respect.
29:12-17	My role in the legal system and elsewhere was to protect the powerless.
29:18-25	It seemed it would always be like that.

29:2-6 HOW HAPPY I WAS UNDER GOD'S PROTECTION!

In earlier times, months and years, I lived under God's protection (cf. 1:10). I was like a man whose companion held a burning lamp up high over our heads, so that we could avoid the rocks on the road. Even though I had grownup sons I was in my prime, a time that is comparable to the days of autumn in nature when, after the summer drought, the fields turn a fresh green again. God's protection was for me like the presence of an old, reliable friend who brought security to the house of my life. With his omnipotence he stood by my side and wherever I appeared my sons surrounded me (cf. Ps. 127:3-5). My business as a farmer flourished so that I could say that I waded, as it were, in the creamy milk of my herds and flocks, while my olive plantations produced streams of olive oil on the rocky ground where they do best.

29:7-11 EVERYONE SHOWED ME RESPECT

Such wealth itself confers a degree of authority on a man. That was very clear when, as one of the family heads, I went to the city for a court session or a deliberative meeting. Such gatherings take place in or by the city gate. A slave followed me to carry the chair on which I would later sit as one of the judges. Boys and men—keen to hear what the tribal heads would decide, not merely out of curiosity, but also in order to learn with a view to a time when they would be called to participate in these meetings—would respectfully step aside for me and, right up to the oldest members of the gathering, would rise from their seats and remain standing till I was seated. Even the high-ranking men in the gathering expected me to speak authoritatively, covering their mouths with their hand as a sign that they would continue to listen to me in silence. Tribal heads, in session, would fall silent when I spoke; it was as if their tongues would stick, in surprise, to the roof of their mouths. After I finished, everyone congratulated me: the right solution had been found. My making an appearance was already enough to insure a consensus.

29:12-17 MY ROLE IN THE LEGAL SYSTEM AND ELSEWHERE WAS TO PROTECT THE POWERLESS

Do not think, however, that my authority rested only, or primarily, on my wealth. I gained the respect of the community by my championing the cause of the disenfranchised—by the boldness with which I dared to oppose the injustice done to the powerless by greedy men of wealth. The person reduced to penury and pressured by the extravagant interest rates charged by men of capital out of the class of landowners did not call in vain for my assistance in the court sessions. That was the experience also of orphans who had no rights in the community, and, in general, of every person who was unable to find an advocate among those in authority. My reward was a "God-bless-you" from the poor, or the smile on the face of the widow who testified to the joy she felt. This is how I understood my role as judge, and the cause of social justice was as close to me, and as familiar, as my own clothing: to see me was to see social justice in action. From tip to toe I was wrapped up in it.

Outside the legal system, also, I was ever prepared to assist the helpless, to guide a blind person by the hand, or to support a cripple with my arm. I cared for the poor as a father cares for his children. I would never say that the needs of strangers did not concern me.

On the contrary, I took time to examine whether they had grounds for complaining about the treatment accorded them and, if they had, I acted publicly in their interest. The scoundrel who, like a predatory animal, tried to snatch away the scant possessions of the poor, had to deal with me and did not get away easily.

29:18-25 IT SEEMED IT WOULD ALWAYS BE LIKE THAT

It never occurred to me that my circumstances would ever change. I thought: As my strength is now, so it will always be until I die. And death seemed so distant I did not have to take account of it, for days as numerous as the grains of sand at the seashore seemed to be my lot. I was as healthy as a tree whose roots continually draw plenty of water from the ground and whose leaves are refreshed by the dew every night. The respect I enjoyed among my fellow citizens renewed itself from day to day. Spiritually I was well armed; my alertness never diminished; it was like a bow that keeps its resilience.

When in the gatherings of the leaders decisions had to be made, they waited for my advice. They were silent in order to hear what my counsel would be. Once I had given my opinion no one wanted to argue against it anymore. Like gentle rain on dry ground, so were my words received in the meetings. To all, my words were as welcome as the final spring showers before the dry season begins. When others did not yet know what to do in one tangled case or another, my smile encouraged them. Then no one tried, by raising objections, to change that smile into a frown. Just as a king chooses the roads on which his armies will march and sits down to let his troops pass muster, so I indicated the direction they had to follow and saw to it that our decisions were carried out. When they were in difficulties my advice was the liberating word that swept away their pessimism. Cheerfully, like persons who had been truly comforted, they went on their way.

JOB DESCRIBES HIS PRESENT STATE OF MISERY 30:1-31

Job's present state, in shrill contrast to his former happiness, is one of unmitigated wretchedness. As against the honor that was formerly accorded him even by people of the highest rank, there is now the scorn with which the lowest of the low treat him. Those people, the pariahs of society, are described even more extensively here than in 24:5-8. They, as well as anyone else of his time, feel free to inflict on him any conceivable dishonor. While formerly the esteem in which he was held was unblemished (29:20), his dignity is now gone—blown away (30:15). Even worse than what people do to him is God's ruthlessness toward him. This is the first time since 17:3-4 that Job speaks directly to God (30:20-23), and he even ventures to compare God's treatment of him with how he himself used to act toward the irremediable misfortune of others (30:2, 25), a comparison that turns out the worse for God. Nowhere does Job find help or comfort.

A number of statements in this chapter present difficult linguistic problems—specifically, for instance, the conclusion of verses 3 and 4, all of verses 12 and 18, and the second half of verse 20. The reader will have to trust that we have done our level best faithfully to reproduce the Hebrew text as it has been handed down to us.

Our subdivisions of this chapter are as follows:

30:1-8   The least of the rabble laugh me to scorn.

30:9-17   Now that God has afflicted me, they show all this daring.

30:18-24   Worse for me than their scorn is God's treatment of me.

30:25-31   I was merciful but you, God, are merciless.

30:1-8 THE LEAST OF THE RABBLE LAUGH
ME TO SCORN

While formerly everyone had respect for me, even the most high-ranking people, I am now being laughed at by young people of the lowest class, people without any background, whose father I disdained to put in charge, together with my dogs, of my sheep and goats. A shepherd has to be able to defend the animals entrusted to him against jackals and more dangerous wild beasts (1 Sam. 17:34-37), but for that purpose they were not strong enough, emaciated as they were from lack of food. They tried to feed themselves with the wild herbs that grow in the dry wastelands (cf. 2 Kings 4:38-41), like the salty leaves of the mallow or the more or less edible leaves of thornbushes. They cooked this inferior food over the woody roots of the broom trees for lack of firewood. With such a diet there is no chance to grow strong. Of course they try to steal some of our field products but as soon as farmers discover such tramps they raise a hue and cry to chase them off and to warn other landowners.

Such people have no place in a well-ordered society. They do not have homes or shelters; they find themselves a place to stay where the winter rains have hollowed out the sides of the wadi (cf. 24:8) or water has carved out a cave that is full of sand and rocks. One can hear the whooping and hollering of such families from between the thornbushes and the high thistles. Of course, they have no code of conduct and no form of behavior is beneath their dignity. They are useless rabble that one ordinarily has to drive away with sticks.

30:9-17 NOW THAT GOD HAS AFFLICTED ME, THEY
SHOW ALL THIS DARING

Now that same kind of scum has the nerve to sing taunt songs at my expense:

> Job, boy, haw haw!
> Belly full of straw, haw!
> Set it on fire;
> Make him squirm,
> Watch him burn,
> Sitting in the mire!

I am the subject of their villainous talk. They now think themselves too good to have anything to do with me and avoid me as somone afflicted by God. When they come close to me they show their loathing by spitting in my face. That is how one keeps his distance from a person who is obviously despised by the powers of heaven. And it is true: while formerly "the bow was ever new in my hand" (29:20), God has left me unstrung and degraded me. They now toy with me at their pleasure.

And not only they! In earlier days I might champion the cause of the defenseless, but now that I am defenseless, no one stands up for me. In my imagination I can see how at the trials in the old style one or more accusers rise up to the right of me (Ps. 109:7; Zech. 3:1). They are men a generation younger than I; a brood I call them, mere birds in the nest, their beaks wide open. The judges let them speak freely, however much they slander me, and I feel like a besieged city against whose wall they throw up siege-ramps in order to be able to roll up their battering rams. They break up the road by which I might escape. Together they have but one goal: my definitive downfall. No one takes up cudgels on my behalf. Already the battering rams have made a wide breach in my wall; they are already storming through the breach, like water bursting through a dam—wave on wave of attackers making a fearful noise.

It is all imagination, you say? But I cannot think straight anymore; all my thoughts are in disarray; I am overwhelmed. My earlier dignity as the richest among my peers has been battered down by the blows of my misfortune. I have lost my freedom to act, my well-being; like a cloud driven by the wind it has evaporated. All I have left is inner confusion and utter weakness, as though I am hemorrhaging inside. My days only bring humiliation, a loss of the high rank I used to enjoy. When I am alone at night and do not hear the voice of my enemies, even then I do not rest. Pain pierces me from the inside; when everything is at rest, pain, like an insatiable worm, keeps gnawing at me.

30:18-24 WORSE FOR ME THAN THEIR SCORN IS GOD'S TREATMENT OF ME

God is like an armed robber who strips me, lonely traveler, of my clothes (cf. Mic. 2:8) and only leaves me a piece of my shirt to cover my shame. He has deprived me of my dignity. Helpless, I lie in the mire, so covered with sand and muck that people cannot tell who I am. I can call to God for help and I do call: to you, God, who have robbed me of everything that was my joy and honor, I call, but you, robber that you are, do not care. When I raise myself with great effort, you look at my thin frame without any pity: I am a curious apparition that does not concern you. I have known you as a generous benefactor but I do not recognize you anymore. I can only see in you a ruthless tyrant who overpowers and mistreats me.

I am like a branch torn off a tree by a whirlwind, swept high into the air and about to fall to the ground in pieces. I have no hope left and I know I shall soon return to the earth, as the ancient word has it (Gen. 3:19): "Dust thou art and unto dust shalt thou return." This, for that matter, is the destination of all living things: they all come together in the realm of the dead. Death is my destination, as it is anyone else's, but why do you make it so hard for me? Once a house has collapsed into a heap of rubble—and what else is my life?— then what is the point of pulling down that heap? You do not have to kick a man who cannot be healed anymore, do you?

30:25-31 I WAS MERCIFUL BUT YOU, GOD, ARE MERCILESS

I, too, have known people in my life who were beyond rescue, but then I conducted myself differently than you conduct yourself toward me. On that, fully conscious of my past, I would dare to swear an oath. I used to weep with those who weep (cf. Rom. 12:15); even though it brought no change, it was comforting to them that someone shared in their lot. But that attitude seems to be foreign to you. You unexpectedly brought suffering into my life and let night fall over my existence. Hot fever rages through my body and does not come to rest. In addition, there is the contempt of my surroundings, which have no regard for my former estate anymore and make me swallow new humiliations and insults. So my life has become a constant round of sorrow and grief. The sun does not shine for me anymore. In former days I was the pillar of the entire community (29:21-25); now I can only stand up in the assembly and cry for help, and that in vain. I no longer feel at home among my fellowmen and fit in much better with the jackals, who make their mournful sounds at night, or with the ostriches, "daughters of the desert," who moan so sorrowfully, as though they had reached the outer limits of sadness (Mic. 1:8). For my part, I have every reason to moan: sickness has blackened my skin and my body burns with fever. The melody of my life, formerly allegro with the tuneful music of harp and flute, has now become shrill and plaintive, like the sounds of mourning and lament (cf. Matt. 11:17).

JOB'S GREAT OATH OF INNOCENCE 31:1-40

If someone in ancient Israel gave property, animate or inanimate, to another for safe-keeping, and the property could not be found later in the possession of that person, the latter had to swear an oath that he had not "laid his hands on the other man's property" (Exod. 22:7-13). Such an oath was regularly required when a position of trust was terminated, as occurred for instance when someone had been appointed as shepherd of a flock and was accused of having sold some of the animals and pocketing the money. By analogy, Samuel the judge, when he laid down his office, could testify and swear before God that he had never taken a bribe (1 Sam. 12:3-5). It is such an oath of innocence that Job here swears at the end of all he had to say.

An oath is a self-imprecation in the event that the oathtaker is lying. One could say, for instance: "God do so to me and more also, if I . . ." (2 Sam. 3:35), the words probably being accompanied by a throat-cutting gesture. Similarly, in this chapter, Job pronounces such a self-imprecation several times (vv. 8, 10, 22, 40). As a rule, however, it was not necessary to utter the self-imprecation, or the writer of the passage in Scripture deemed it undesirable to use such severe language. Usually it was thought sufficient to pronounce just the protasis: "If I have done this or that, then . . ." or, "If I have not done this or that, then. . . ." So the simple conjunction "if" served as a denial under oath; the same conjunction followed by a denial—"if not"—became a confirmation with an oath. To indicate that in such cases we are dealing with an oath we have replaced the "if" with: "I swear: I have never . . ."; the "if not" with: "I swear, I have always. . . ."

If a person were accused of many improper actions it was his duty to deny each one with a separate oath. The order of the oaths followed the order of the accusations. They might come from several directions and one need not look for any systematic order. No such order can be discovered in the series of oaths that Job utters in this chapter. The count, taken strictly, is fourteen, but in the arrangement offered here we have taken several of them together. The sections are still unequal in length; we could not avoid it. In some cases Job adds to the oath an explanation of why he has not done certain things—or, conversely, why he has (vv. 2-4, 11-12, 14-15, 18, 23, 28); but not in every instance.

One might think that every one of Job's oaths contained a denial of unrighteous acts of which he was accused by his friends. These friends have in fact suggested that he in all likelihood committed a variety of acts of social injustice. But Job also denied involvement in matters that his friends have not mentioned, such as sexual sins (vv. 1, 9) and idolatry (vv. 26-28). Without any system whatever, sins against God and sins against one's neighbor follow each other in the list. It is worth reporting here that in Job's denial of taking pleasure in other people's pain (vv. 29-30), the ancient Aramaic version (see Introduction, under I.1 and passim) had two verses (four lines) more than the present Hebrew text. Unfortunately, these lines occur in a badly damaged part of the scroll, so that it is impossible to give a translation.

It has often been thought that verses 38-40 have been put in the wrong location. Some have attempted to move them to a variety of other places in the series of oaths. It is certainly true that verses 35-37 would serve beautifully as the impressive conclusion of the whole and that the following, and final, oath (vv. 38-40), to our mind, forms an anticlimax after the challenging verses 35-37, but no consensus has been reached concerning the place where they should then be inserted and the Aramaic version just referred to has these verses in the same location as the Hebrew. So we shall just leave them there.

With some hesitation we shall divide this chapter in the following pericopes:

31:1-6   I have never looked at a virgin with lustful eyes.
31:7-12   Nor have I seduced my neighbor's wife.
31:13-23   I was just and kind toward inferiors.
31:24-28   I have idolized neither gold nor the celestial bodies.
31:29-30   I took no pleasure in another person's pain.
31:31-32   I never refused hospitality to anyone.
31:33-37   I was, and still am, an upright man.
31:38-40   I treated my laborers fairly.

31:1-6 I HAVE NEVER LOOKED AT A VIRGIN WITH LUSTFUL EYES

Just as a king rules over his vassals and lays certain obligations on them, so I stayed on top of my senses and did not cast lustful glances at any young girl, however attractive she might be. I was very well aware that such activity, by divine arrangement, only results in misery, not only for the girl but also for myself: God would not let it go unpunished; he would bring evil upon me and assign to me all kinds of miseries as a sin-laden inheritance. I will never deny the fact that God knows how to find out the evildoer and pays out to him what he has coming. All sin avenges itself on earth. God has carefully scrutinized the entire conduct of my life from day to day and has kept a precise step-by-step account of my deeds. Fully conscious of the fact that I have never ventured on devious paths, I am prepared to declare on oath that I am pure. I have never sweet-talked a girl into bed with me; I have never deceived one with false promises. Many nations picture the justice of heaven with the image of balances in the hands of the deity. Let God weigh me—with my declaration of innocence—and put truth on the other side of the scales: he will not find me too light.

31:7-12 NOR HAVE I SEDUCED MY NEIGHBOR'S WIFE

I swear that I have never departed from the path of decency, nor pursued the desire of my eyes; and that I have kept my hands, like my heart, clean. Should that be untrue, then may God decree that the harvest of my fields be taken and consumed by my enemies, and that the early growth be torn out and destroyed by them.

To speak plainly: I swear that I have never in my heart coveted my neighbor's wife nor ever followed the devious behavior of adulterers. They keep their eyes fixed on the door of their neighbor's house, and when they have seen the husband leave in the morning to work in the fields, they sneak into the same door to seduce the wife. Never in my life have I done anything like this! Should that be untrue, then may God act with me according to the law of retribution, an eye for an eye and a tooth for a tooth: may he turn my wife into the least of the female slaves (cf. Exod. 11:5), make her the legal property of her master for the satisfaction of his lusts, and even let her be hired out to other men for the same purpose—to my shame and sorrow.

People rightly speak of a relationship with another man's wife as a disgrace and when it happens the injured husband can take it before the judges with a demand that it be punished in accordance with law: the death penalty for both (Lev. 20:10). Adultery is a hellish fire that consumes everything; it is like a fire in a field of grain, which burns deeply into the ground (cf. Amos 7:4) and does not spare the roots of the crop just sown, so that new shoots cannot come up anymore. Adultery affects the roots of a man's existence. As an ancient wise man has said: "Can a man carry fire in his bosom and his clothes not be burned? Or can one walk upon hot coals and his feet not be scorched? So is he who goes in to his neighbor's wife" (Prov. 6:27-29).

31:13-23 I WAS JUST AND KIND TOWARD INFERIORS

According to the law of God, slaves, both male (Exod. 21:2-6, 26-27; Deut. 15:12-18) and female (Exod. 21:7-11), have rights in relation to their master and owner. I have always honored those rights. I knew that, if I were to deny such voiceless people access to law, God himself would arise as judge and call me to account (cf. Jer. 34:8-22). If he were to examine the issue I would not be able to defend myself. When it comes to justice before God, slave and owner are equal. Both have been created by him, formed under his all-embracing rule in the womb.

So I was also generous toward the poor, people who, though free in name, are dependent on the benevolence of the rich for their existence. I swear: no one ever asked me for help in vain; I never let a widow, looking faint from hunger, go without helping her. Orphans got their share from my dinner table; I never ate alone with them looking on hungrily. How could I? God himself had always cared for me as a father and could I then let his other children go hungry?

When some poor tramp without decent clothing came to my door for shelter, I would give him a woolen blanket from my supplies; and he would leave saying "Thank you!" and "God bless you!" because he could finally keep his body warm and comfortable. To that, too, I could swear an oath!

I never violated the rights of an orphan by depriving him of his lawful inheritance. Sure—I could have done it, for he had no legal helper who could have resisted me in the gate where court sessions are held, and as a respected man in the community I could always count on the support of my fellow citizens—but I did not do it. Should that be untrue, then may God cause my whole arm, which I raised against an orphan, to drop off by cancer or accident, in accordance with the inexorable law of retribution! It just did not occur to me to injure an orphan, for I have always known that God would wreak vengeance on me by sending misfortune, and the kind of misfortune at that, against which even the most powerful person on earth would be powerless. I would refrain from an unjust and cruel action against orphans out of self-interest—from fear of the punitive majesty of God—supposing now that by nature and temperament I were capable of such action, which I am not.

31:24-28 I HAVE IDOLIZED NEITHER GOLD NOR THE CELESTIAL BODIES

From one's store of precious metals one can make an idol (cf. Judg. 17:1-6). But there are also more subtle forms of idolatry in the world. The moment one puts his trust in his supply of gold instead of in God's providence, one has already made an idol of the gold. But there is an even more subtle possibility: when the increase of one's possessions is one's chief source of satisfaction in life, then that is already a form of idolatry. I swear I have not been guilty of any of these.

Nor have I, in imitation of so much that is practiced around us, made for myself a sun-god or moon-god of the sun and moon, both of them creations of God, however beautiful they are. While pagans, the moment they see the sun rise or the moon appear, at least throw them a kiss, I have never felt a temptation to do it, I swear, either privately or in public. For that would be to deny the Creator; one would adore the creature instead of the Creator and so commit a punishable offense, to be expiated in Israel before a popular court, outside of Israel before the judgment seat of God.

31:29-30 I TOOK NO PLEASURE IN ANOTHER PERSON'S PAIN

I know: there are people who regard pleasure over another's pain the best of pleasures, but I never got a thrill from seeing someone else's misfortune, not even if it was my worst enemy. For that reason I never uttered a curse against a personal enemy to help bring about his misfortune. Had I done that, I would have commited a sin of the mouth (cf., however, 2 Sam. 16:5-14) and been coresponsible, at least morally, for his death. Again I swear: I have never committed such a verbal sin.

31:31-32 I NEVER REFUSED HOSPITALITY TO ANYONE

When a stranger came to my door I would invite him to my dinner table and he could share in the roast prepared by my wife or slave (cf. Gen. 18:1-8). The traveler passing by, even if he were a complete stranger and belonged to a clan or nation other than my own, could always count on overnight shelter (cf. Gen. 19:1-3 in contrast with Judg. 19:15). Both wings of the front door of my big house would always be open to travelers. That was something very different from the charity shown to the poor, something I swore to a moment ago (v. 17). They really needed me to be kind to them, but the travelers as a rule had their own tents and food supply with them (cf. Judg. 19:19). But I never said, "They can take care of themselves!" For me it was an honor and a joy to offer hospitality to strangers. To that, also, I can swear an oath with a relaxed mind.

31:33-37 I WAS, AND STILL AM, AN UPRIGHT MAN

Perhaps people think: "He makes all these statements and no one can prove that in secret he ever committed any of the sins he has denied committing," but I have to say that it was my nature to be upright. It is entirely human, from a fear of what the people will say or of what will make the rounds in the larger circle of the clans, to hide one's wrongdoings; to keep them concealed, so to speak, in the folds of one's robe where the money or other precious things are kept. Being thus filled with a sense of unworthiness, people become paranoid; they do not talk with anyone or step outdoors anymore. But in my case there was not a trace of this kind of behavior, for the simple reason that I had nothing whatever to hide.

For that reason I wish that someone were willing to listen as a judge to the oath of innocence I have uttered, and you will understand that in saying this I am referring to God. I submit this series of oaths to the supreme Judge in writing, as it were, as a writ marked with my own seal, and I am excited to know what he who knows all things, even hidden sins, could possibly enter against any of my oaths. God is my Adversary: let him submit a counterplea! Perhaps you ask how I can regard one and the same God as both Judge and Adversary. You must know how it goes at the court of a great king, a ruler of a world empire. He has many vassals, rulers of smaller kingdoms subject to him. If he suspects that one of them is disloyal, this vassal is summoned to the capital, and there a court session is held in which the great king is both judge and accuser. I am God's vassal, powerful in my own domain, but at the same time his servant (1:8, etc.). God acts as my Adversary but is at the same time my Judge.

So let me see what God can say against my oaths in a counterplea. Such a document would be most welcome to me for it could only confirm my innocence. When it is handed to me I will not hide it in the folds of my robe, but drape it over my shoulder so that anyone who wants to can read it, or even wrap it around my forehead like a wreath. It will serve me as an ornament, for it will prove that God is unable to accuse me of anything essential. Of my entire conduct throughout the years I can give an account—without fear. Like a prince who is unafraid of his opponent, I shall watch him come near to position himself at my right hand (30:12), the traditional place of the accuser.

31:38-40 I TREATED MY LABORERS FAIRLY

O yes: there is one possible accusation I almost forgot! I have described my conduct toward my male and female slaves, as well as that toward the poor, widows, and orphans, but in the interest of completeness I also want to swear an oath that I have never dealt dishonorably or unfairly with my hired fieldworkers. If it were otherwise, my own fields, speaking figuratively, would cry out against me: the furrows would appear, weeping, before the judge. But I never profited from the harvest of my lands without paying the laborers the wages coming to them (cf., by contrast, James 5:4) and I gave them the necessary food and drink while they were working for me (cf. Rev. 2:14). If in this respect I am perjuring myself, then may the grain never grow in my fields, but only thornbushes and other weeds!

ELIHU JOINS IN THE DISCUSSION 32:1-5

In the Introduction (I.5) we have already asserted that chapters 32-37 must be the work of a wisdom teacher who lived approximately a century later than the poet of Job. He begins by saying that the three friends have stopped answering Job because Job stubbornly insisted that he was right. Next he introduces Elihu, whose name is borne by various persons in the Old Testament but who cannot be identified with any one of them. We should not attempt to interpret his name—which means "my God is he"—symbolically, for then we would also have to find symbolic explanations for the names Barakel, Buz, and Ram, which, concerning the last two, we cannot do. In the Old Testament Barakel only occurs in this pericope but in some Babylonian documents it occurs as the name of a Jewish merchant. The name Buz occurs in Genesis 22:21, next to that of Uz, which is Job's country; perhaps that is the source from which the wisdom teacher took the name. Since in Job Uz refers to a country, we also take Buz that way. The name Ram is also that of one of David's ancestors (Ruth 4:19) but here it refers not to an Israelite clan but to a demographic group that lived in or near the land of Uz, as the ancient Greek translation also has it: "in the Uzzite land." The description of Elihu's origins is much more extensive than that of Job's relatives or of the three friends—another indication that these chapters were not written by the poet of the book as a whole.

Elihu is dissatisfied with Job and his three friends, but for different reasons: with Job, for presuming to insist on his rights against God; with the three friends, for being unable to refute Job's arguments. One must not think, therefore, that Elihu is taking a position in the middle; he stands totally on God's side in his protest against Job's statements and only charges the friends that they have failed to find the proper arguments against Job.

Elihu waited to speak until Job had finished (cf. 31:40). The words of Job were answers to what the three friends had put forward. Elihu did not want to speak before all this had been fully dealt with because he was so much younger. First the dialogue among the older men had to be finished; that was a matter of protocol. Now that they have all stopped speaking Elihu can air his dissatisfaction. He does this in four consecutive discourses.

ELIHU'S FIRST DISCOURSE 32:6–33:33

The first thing that strikes the reader is the expansiveness of Elihu's introduction to his proposed discourse (32:6–33:7). In keeping with the wordy beginning is the repetition of the same key words. The word *pit* occurs five times in 33:18-30; the poet of the earlier discourses would certainly have drawn from his rich vocabulary equivalents like "grave," "Sheol," "destruction" and "underworld." Furthermore, the invitation to listen to him is repeated in 32:10; 33:1; 33:31 and 33, each time with the use of the same verb.

Another difference between the wisdom teacher's work and that of the poet of the rest is that in Elihu's speeches the name Job, whether in the vocative (in this part 33:1 and

33:31) or in another case form (32:12), occurs repeatedly; this is not true in the preceding three rounds of discourses.

Elihu starts out on a very modest note (32:6-7) but in the course of his address he gains more and more self-confidence, so that in 32:18-20 his language sounds positively prophetic (cf. Jer. 20:9). Although he does not say so in so many words, it is pretty clear that, in referring to the "angel" who intercedes for the sufferer who then gets better and shouts with joy (33:23-28), Elihu has himself in mind and hence views himself as "one out of a thousand." We should notice that his section shows an unusual structure: twice two verses of three lines, followed by the ordinary verse-form of two lines, as though Elihu were giving a song in two similar strophes. The device of a verse in three lines is sometimes used when something unusually important needs to be said, and in fact this piece is the only one in which Elihu offers an insight that has not been expressed before: the redemptive function of intercession (cf. James 5:14-16).

Of Elihu's first discourse we present the following outline:

32:6-12	The speeches of the friends were not convincing.
32:13-17	Now I come with stronger arguments.
32:18-22	I am forced to speak by inner compulsion.
33:1-7	I speak to Job as man to man.
33:8-13	Job has no right to blame God.
33:14-22	By his word and chastening God would teach man submissiveness.
33:23-28	But then he shows him compassion.
33:29-33	Take this, and the remainder of what I have to say, to heart.

32:6-12 THE SPEECHES OF THE FRIENDS WERE NOT CONVINCING

First I wish to say a word to Job's friends who now have nothing left to say. You are two or three times older than I; for that reason I did not venture to take part in your conversation with Job. I believed your experience and knowledge of the wisdom you inherited from earlier generations would enable you to say the redeeming word, but I am disappointed. So I experienced again that age does not necessarily bring wisdom, as Job himself also indicated (12:2). Wisdom is a gift conferred upon the children of men only by the operation of the Spirit of God; only he who has God's breath in him can understand the riddles that perplex others. Age and grey hairs do not by themselves guarantee insight, any more than majorities are always right. And so, though there are three of you and I am alone, and though you are men of advanced age and I am only a novice, I make bold to ask Job to listen to what I have to say. You cannot accuse me of a lack of modesty, for I have listened long and attentively to the words of eloquence you spoke, but what I did not hear was a refutation of Job's arguments and after his great concluding discourse (chaps. 29-31) you had nothing left to say.

32:13-17 NOW I COME WITH STRONGER ARGUMENTS

If I were to remain silent you would be able to say that you had found the key to Job's enigmatic lot: namely, that God as supreme Judge had found his accusations unacceptable and ejected him from before his judgment seat (cf. Acts 18:16). But for all your insinuations that Job has committed great sins and so deserved his suffering, you have not proved a thing nor brought him around to repentance. On the contrary, a moment ago he pronounced his great oath of innocence, and in response you said nothing. To me he has not said anything and I will not repeat what you have said to him. So I am going to address the issue afresh and approach it from an entirely different direction. Your three friends, Job, are tongue-tied and have given up arguing with you. As I said, now that they are silent, there is no reason for me to defer speech. Now I want to put in my "two cents' worth" and have my say.

32:18-22 I AM FORCED TO SPEAK
BY INNER COMPULSION

I have much to say. Job's statements have so stirred me up I am close to exploding. My insides are full of it. Like grape juice that has begun to ferment, so I am in a state of fermentation. If the gas bubbles cannot find a way out, accidents happen: new wine tends to burst the bags made of goatskin in which it was put too soon (cf. Matt. 9:17). I feel like the prophet in Israel who tried to hold in the word God had given him to speak, but it became a burning fire in his heart; he exhausted himself suppressing it but he could not (Jer. 20:9). It will be a great relief to me to formulate my thoughts; I will no longer clamp my lips together. Job's words demand a refutation.

I will not take sides, either with Job or with his friends; I will flatter no one. I have never learned to address high dignitaries with all the proper titles. I simply say what I have to say. The God who gave me life and charged me, like that ancient prophet, with a message would, if I would pull such rhetorical stunts, instantly disavow me; worse, he would summon me, as an unfaithful messenger, before the heavenly court.

33:1-7 I SPEAK TO JOB AS MAN TO MAN

That much, then, to the friends; from now on I will only address myself to you, Job, and ask for your full attention. Please note carefully what I have to say, for I am now starting my speech to you. I will tell you honestly what is in my heart. I will say exactly what God has given me to say: it is knowledge from him, his message. It is by the working of God's Spirit that I am what I am; his breath animates and inspires me.

In speaking to you, Job, I do not wish to put myself on a higher moral level than you; if you have any fault to find with my discourse, please say it. Take your stand in the ring with me! In God's eye we are both just human beings, completely equal. To say it the Babylonian way: the Creator took a handful of clay and nipped off two pieces; of the one he made me, of the other, you. That is the reason why you do not have to let yourself feel overwhelmed by me; I do not presume to have authority with which to crush you. What I want, and expect from you, is a reasonable discussion.

33:8-13 JOB HAS NO RIGHT TO BLAME GOD

I have to say, first of all, that you have spoken rather too boldly about God; your words upset me, and it is as if I am still hearing them. Over and over you kept saying you were blameless (9:21; 10:7; 16:17; 23:10; 27:6) and you have sworn to it by your great oath of innocence (chap. 31). You conveyed to us that God was looking for a pretext—some little occasion or other—to raise a storm against you, as he did against the

Philistines long ago (Judg. 14:4), and you have expressly said that God regarded you as his enemy (13:24; 19:11). To quote you literally (13:27), you charged that God "fastened your feet in shackles" like a slave and never gave you a moment's freedom to go your own way.

But I think that is going too far, and on that point you are definitely wrong, for that is not the way to speak about God, the infinitely high God, before whom all of us are mere earthworms. This kind of speech betrays a lack of respect for God and it is plain that, when you speak about God as you do, you have lost sight of the submissiveness that behooves us as human beings before God. You act as though you were God's equal. You lodge a complaint against him the way a man indicts a fellow citizen before the courts when he thinks himself injured. But God is not your fellow citizen and you seem to forget that. Beside a lack of submissiveness I also see in such behavior a grand lack of good sense, for God does not let himself be called to account for his administration. When a person like yourself proceeds to do it anyway, he will only meet with solid silence.

33:14-22 BY HIS WORD AND CHASTENING GOD WOULD TEACH MAN SUBMISSIVENESS

That is not to say that God is always silent. He does speak to a person but not because that person could force him to. When God speaks he speaks on his own initiative and in a way that allows him to remain God, The Invisible One, who lives in unapproachable light (cf. 1 Tim. 1:17; 6:16). To that end he uses two means.

In the first place he can send a man a dream. Not all dreams are deceptive; when God wants to speak to man through a dream he does it by a vision in the night, such as came to Jacob at Bethel (Gen. 28:10-15). It is not so long ago that the Israelite prophet Zechariah told of eight visions that came to him consecutively (Zech. 1:7–6:8). So God can and does speak to people; his warnings, by which he steers them back on the right path, then have the force of a document on which his seal has been stamped. In this way the distance between God and man is kept intact, a practice which is good for man, for if God were to appear to him in his naked majesty he would die. Such indirect speech of God is a great benefit for the one to whom it comes, for without such correction the person would probably continue to sin until he was carried to his grave, a victim of the vengeance of people he had mistreated.

The second means by which God speaks is affliction. A man has lived a wild life, say, but God corrects him through illness. In that case the organs of his body are at war with each other. His appetite, to which he used to give rather free reign, is gone; even the most glorious dish with which his wife wanted to treat him would only make him want to throw up. His overweight condition would soon become skeletal, so that his bones, which were formerly well covered with flesh and fat but are now hardly covered even with skin, stick out of his rump. It seems this illness will drag him, the senseless victim of the power of death, to his grave.

33:23-28 BUT THEN HE SHOWS HIM COMPASSION

That lingering illness, however, is also a message from God. It is a matter of reading it right. God may speak to a man through his suffering but who will explain to him what God is saying? That message must be rendered in human language. Happy is the man to whom a messenger from God appears, as I have come to you, to make God's intentions for you clear and intelligible. There are not many who can do that, at best one out of a thousand. As a genuine prophet he is not only content to warn that God wants the sufferer to experience his helplessness, and so to teach him to be submissive, but he also fulfills his task as an intercessor. He prays, on behalf of the sufferer, that God may have mercy and he indicates to God that the goal of the chastening, humility and submissiveness, has now been achieved. Submissiveness is the ransom to be paid and the ransom has now been found. Now he can return to health and be strong again.

The intercessor begs God to show compassion to the patient and to let him go up to God's house in health again (cf. 2 Kings 20:5, 8). Health is God's great gift and of this gift the restored sufferer sings in the company of the devout who have gathered in the courts of God (cf. Ps. 66:16). He recognizes that by this chastening experience God has made him aware of his shortcomings toward God and men and thanks God that he has put grace above law. Now that he has been spared from death he begins truly to realize that he must be humbly grateful to God for the rest of his life.

33:29-33 TAKE THIS, AND THE REMAINDER OF WHAT I HAVE TO SAY, TO HEART

Under the dispensation of God's providence it happens to a human being a couple of times in a lifetime that after he has been deathly ill, the light of life is restored to him. This very thing may happen to you if you will humbly listen to what God wants to tell you and I have explained to you. Can you advance anything against it? Then do it! It is really not my idea to win an argument. If you can really raise an objection that holds water, I will be glad to let you persuade me. But you are silent? Then I will proceed, for there is still much for me to say and for you to learn.

ELIHU'S SECOND DISCOURSE 34:1-37

The author who inserted Elihu's discourses into the Book of Job does not allow Job to reply to any of them. That is not hard to understand: in that case he would have to put into Job's mouth words that in his opinion were blasphemous, and it is precisely in this second discourse that he expressly protests against such statements of the sufferer. Elihu is not concerned to prove that Job is being punished for sins he possibly committed earlier; his concern is over Job's present sin: his total lack of submission to God's providential arrangements. Job seems to think that, in his government of the world, God should conduct himself in accord with Job's views of right and wrong (v. 33). That kind of language is intolerable; in his protests against it Elihu, both at the beginning of his second discourse (vv. 2-4) and at the end (vv. 34-37), appeals to his listeners as intelligent people. We who read this tend to think that these listeners must be the three friends, but Elihu was not in agreement with them, either (32:3, 5, 6-16). So we must believe he is addressing wise men in general, the readers of the long interpolation, chapters 32-37.

Despite his wordiness Elihu is not entirely clear in this discourse. There are a number of places in it where a trans-

lation and interpretation other than our own is conceivable
(vv. 23, 29, 31, 27). These uncertainties do not, however, affect
the course of the argument.

The argument, in outline, runs as follows:

34:2-9	Let us examine whether Job has spoken rightly.
34:10-16	God does not act unjustly.
34:17-22	God is not partial even to the most powerful.
34:23-30	God has no need for a long preliminary investigation.
34:31-37	Job is lacking in submissiveness to God.

34:2-9 LET US EXAMINE WHETHER JOB HAS SPOKEN RIGHTLY

I make an appeal to all people who are truly wise and have
knowledge of the ways of God. Just as when we eat we can
tell immediately whether the food is sweet or sour, salty or
flat, so an intelligent person listening to a speaker can tell in
seconds whether or not what he says really holds water. We
have heard what Job had to offer; now let us examine the
question whether he had a right to speak as he did. He was
convinced he was right and did not hide that conviction (13:18
and elsewhere); he claimed that God had denied him justice
(27:2) and brought undeserved suffering over him (cf. 6:4;
16:13).

That language is, to us, unheard of; no pious person has
ever spoken like that. It seems he takes pleasure in leveling
his accusations against God; he makes himself drunk on his
own words, words that we can only call a mockery of God's
justice. If he continues along this line we shall soon see him
making common cause with people who want nothing to do
with God or his commandments. Certainly, he is pursuing a
very dangerous line of thought if he denies the usefulness of
a pious way of life. True, he has not said this in so many
words, but this conclusion inevitably follows from his arguments (cf. 9:22; 21:7-15).

34:10-16 GOD DOES NOT ACT UNJUSTLY

Again I make my appeal to everyone who has listened to Job
with discriminating ears. Now listen to me and decide who

is right, Job or I. I want to say emphatically from the depths of my heart: it is unthinkable that God should have anything to do with injustice, or that he would not act in the strictest justice. He rewards the person who does good; he punishes the person who does evil. It is a person's very own way of life that decides his fate, whether for good or ill. He who does good meets with good; he who does evil meets with ill; and all this happens under the just dispensations of God who upholds his laws as an incorruptible judge. Why should he act differently? Since he is the Almighty he has no need to twist justice to his own advantage. The world is his domain; he has created it and does not have to curry the favor of anyone higher than himself. What he in his justice wishes to accomplish for good or ill is not limited by what his power permits. All that is, is dependent on him; sovereignly he rules over all that lives. If he were to set himself in opposition to this world, then everything and everyone would perish. Therefore, I say again: God has no interest in injustice; he is not like a human being who sometimes gets into a situation in which, to protect himself, he has to hurt others. Let the intelligent listener pay attention to my words!

34:17-22 GOD IS NOT PARTIAL EVEN TO THE MOST POWERFUL

It is justice that cements a society together. Would God, then, who holds the universe together, have an aversion to justice? Or do you, Job, want to condemn God on grounds of injustice supposedly done to you by him, and so place yourself above him who is the epitome of power and justice? In his inexorable justice God does not spare even kings or noblemen; if they are no good he addresses them, not with titles given them by man, but with the description they deserve: "scoundrel," "rogue"!

He does not restrict himself to the spoken word, either. There is not a chance in the world that he would take their side if they had committed an injustice, be it to the least of their subjects. For him the highest-ranking people and the very least are absolutely equal; they are all his creatures and therefore subject to his rule. So we observe how those who have been placed in positions of power and misuse them, suddenly, in the middle of the night when there is not a thing people can do, breathe out their last breath—and this is his doing. He only has to touch "his lordship"—and he dies. Apart from any human act of violence this powerful person is whisked away.

He knows what every person does; a mortal cannot take a step that he does not notice. For him the darkness does not exist. As a psalmist has said: "Even the darkness is not dark to thee, the night is bright as the day" (Ps. 139:12).

34:23-30 GOD HAS NO NEED FOR A LONG PRELIMINARY INVESTIGATION

Therefore a person cannot say: "For the time being I shall follow my own will and not worry about God's judgment. Later I shall set a time at which I shall appear before his judgment seat, and before I go I will repair whatever wrong I have done." From moment to moment God knows what people do and does not need to make a long legal investigation. With swift justice unjust rulers are taken away in death at God's command and others are appointed in their place. From this we can tell, as I said a minute ago, that God continually watches the actions of violent men in positions of power, and when people least expect it, in the middle of the night so to speak, he inflicts a catastrophe on them and so brings an end to their criminal activities. This kind of crook is unexpectedly put to death. So it is even described in a psalm: "How they are destroyed in a moment, swept away utterly by terrors!" (Ps. 73:19). Their executions take place in public, as the law provides, so that everyone can see that God is just in his judgment.

Result and purpose are the same for God. So I can say that under God's rule this is the sense of their transgression of God's laws: the downtrodden man, denied his rights by the powerful, lodges a complaint against them before God; God, as Judge, takes notice of his accusation, accepts it as properly before his court, pronounces judgment, and promptly carries out the verdict. God permits men of violence to sin in order, in a moment, to demonstrate his punitive justice upon them (cf. Rom. 9:17, 22). When God refrains from intervening for a time, and seems to watch it from the sidelines, we must wait; there is nothing else we can do for no one other than God can inflict judgment on the mighty. If he hides his face from the poor who complain, and lets matters take their course for a time, because in his opinion the measure of the sins of the tyrants is not yet full (cf. Gen. 15:16), then one has to acquiesce and not, like you, Job, complain that God hides himself (23:8-9). God knows exactly when to act and we should let him take his time, assured that he knows very well what a given nation or person is doing in the way of injustice. He will take care that such harsh rulers will not last long, not letting them plunge the people in their trust into one catastrophe after another over and over (cf. Exod. 10:7).

34:31-37 JOB IS LACKING IN SUBMISSIVENESS TO GOD

It is that kind of submissiveness to God, the kind that springs from the assurance that he knows when to intervene, that I miss in you, Job. God may have his reasons for a period of watchful waiting, reasons we do not know.

Say, for example, that such a tyrant should repent and turn to God in prayer, saying that he both deserves and accepts punishment, and promising that he will refrain from further violence. Perhaps he used to think that as king there were no restrictions on his behavior; but now he humbly asks God for instruction from his law in order to learn that his own insights and views are not the highest standard. He promises amendment of life—must God then still inflict punishment? What can God want that is better than a sinner who repents (cf. Luke 15:7, 10)? You, with your high moral consciousness, want to see bloody retribution imposed on human wrong. You disapprove of the unjust actions of persons in power; are you also going to disapprove of their repentance? Do you prefer vengeance over mercy—the mercy that follows confession and the promise of amendment? That may be your choice, it is not mine! Now tell us what you think!

You are silent? Then I again make my appeal to those who really have insight in the ways of God. They will agree with me that you are totally lacking in the true wisdom that is humble submission to God's government of the universe. It will be their wish that you will be tested further, now that you have adopted such a self-assured and haughty attitude. Your three friends have assumed that in your life you have committed some kind of sin or other. Whether that is true I will leave open, but all decent-minded people will agree with my judgment that what you have said is the language of the impious, language against which I warned you just now (vv.

7-8). So, to the sin your friends have assumed, you now add sin that is manifest to everyone; we have all witnessed how you poured out a flood of unfitting words against God.

ELIHU'S THIRD DISCOURSE 35:1-16

The third discourse of Elihu is the shortest of all four; it is not clear to us why the author of this long interpolation (chaps. 32-37) has made Elihu's speeches of such unequal length. This chapter does not present many difficulties, as only verse 15 offers uncertainty in translation and interpretation. The general idea is this: Godly or ungodly behavior does not make God greater or less; should one wish to invoke his judgment as a judge, one should ask for it as a favor, acknowledging the benefits he has bestowed on us.

We shall divide this chapter in two halves of almost equal length:

35:2-8   The actions of man, whether just or unjust, affect man for better or worse, not God.
35:9-16   An appeal to God must be made in the proper spirit.

35:2-8 THE ACTIONS OF MAN, WHETHER JUST OR UNJUST, AFFECT MAN FOR BETTER OR WORSE, NOT GOD

Do you think, Job, that you have the right to maintain your position against God? Do you really believe that you can bring your case before God in that manner, in a case that is even against God? You presumed to say some time ago (34:9) that a man abstains from sin pointlessly (cf. Ps. 73:13-14). I mention that again because I see in it your biggest mistake. I want to respond to it; and my response is aimed not only at you but also at your new friends, the ungodly, against whose companionship I have seriously warned you already in my previous discourse (34:8-9).

Direct your eyes once, not toward yourself and your fellow human beings, but toward the heavens! You see the clouds floating there; they go on floating, no matter what you do, whether you act piously or use the most ungodly language.

Your behavior neither helps nor hurts them. That is how it is with God; he remains himself, however much or often you sin. Similarly, God has no need of your piety or righteousness; it does not enhance him, it does not bring him any personal advantage. The actions of man, whether just or unjust, affect only man for better or worse.

35:9-16 AN APPEAL TO GOD MUST BE MADE IN THE PROPER SPIRIT

The misuse of power—the practice of extortion—occurs everywhere and often. People in high places, as well as the rich, use their position in society to advance their own interests at the expense of justice and mercy. It is quite understandable that the oppressed, in his powerless position, should seek redress and assistance from God—but then that should be done in the right spirit.

One can cry out "Where is God?" for the purpose of seeing him intervene, but the very first thing in prayer has to be the acknowledgment of God's sovereignty, the sovereignty of him who is the Creator of all men, also of the man who prays to him, who must therefore approach him reverently. The second point to remember in such prayer is gratitude for the benefits God grants also to the poor: every night he confers new strength on him through the gift of sleep; even to the lowliest human being he has given the intelligence that lifts him far above the animals. Humble gratitude for such gifts has to be expressed before one asks for other things.

But what do we see? People instantly demand their rights; they stand upon their rights as though one can make demands of God. That is nothing but pride! God owes us nothing, and by acting so ungratefully and presumptuously toward God, the poor man puts himself on one level with the oppressors who imagine in their way that God is automatically on their side. Oppressors and oppressed: they are all self-assured sinners. One must not think that God answers such prayers. But the right content—humility and gratitude—is lacking in them.

So far I have spoken in general, but what I am saying also applies to you, Job, and to your impetuous prayers to God. You insult him if you charge that so far he has not taken up your cause. If you had had recourse to an earthly judge you would have waited patiently till it pleased him to take notice of your case. It behooves you to assume the same attitude toward God: you ought to have waited patiently and in trust till God decided the moment had come to pay attention to your complaint. But now that you are not ready to assume that attitude you have incurred God's anger; the Judge, whom you have insulted, wants nothing to do with a man who addresses him in such vehement language, a person who rattles on like a Chaldean chariot.

Therefore I completely agree with the conclusion that my listeners drew at the end of my second discourse (34:34-37): all those inflated words of Job get him nowhere; they only prove that he does not know in what state of mind it is proper for a human being to come to God.

ELIHU'S FOURTH DISCOURSE 36:1–37:24

Elihu's fourth discourse is the longest of all. For us it is also the most difficult, and that for two reasons. For one thing, it contains numerous linguistic puzzles, for example in 36:14, 16, 17, 33; 37:10, 20. Our translation and interpretation of these verses differs considerably from the usual and we do not claim absolute validity for them. In the second place, it is hard to find one continuous line of argument in this long speech. It can still be done in 36:2-23 where Elihu declares that God, in his just government, punishes evildoers and calls the haughty to repentance, a speech that ends with a personal warning to Job. So it seems Elihu is saying that human beings can find reasons why God acts as he does; but from 36:24 to 37:24 Elihu praises God's inscrutable activity in nature, which surpasses all human understanding: there are no reasons to be found for it.

So it is with some reserve that we offer the following outline:

36:2-7   God governs all things with wisdom and righteousness.
36:8-15   By chastening them God brings the haughty to repentance.
36:16-23 Prosperity can also be your downfall.
36:24-33 Remember: God's government is unsearchable.
37:1-13   Consider God's greatness in nature.

37:14-24   God's work far exceeds our powers of com-
            prehension.

36:2-7 GOD GOVERNS ALL THINGS WITH
WISDOM AND RIGHTEOUSNESS

I have already said much, Job, but there is much more to say
in defense of God. So please bear with me a while longer.
What I know is not my own invention but has come down to
us from distant ancestors. Just as our forefathers spoke, so I
will also speak to uphold God's right. You consider yourself
wronged by him who has created us all, but I want to speak
on behalf of God's righteousness in his government of the
world. I assure you that in my speech I will not draw on my
own conceptions. I shall let the facts speak for themselves,
and the weightiest fact is that if you appear with a complaint
against God, you get to deal with someone who knows and
fathoms all things—including your secret sins and most hidden thoughts.

   God is not only all-knowing but also all-powerful. For
that reason he never has to recant or recall anything. Wisdom
and power are one in him; his knowledge is his power. So
we observe in his government of the world that he punishes
the evildoer with death, sooner or later, and that he restores
to their rightful position the lowly who have been oppressed
by ruthless men of power. Again: it happens sooner or later,
for he may have his reasons for letting the rascals first make
full the measure of their wickedness. Meanwhile, he does not
lose sight of the decent and upright man. In God's good time
the tables will turn and then the lowly person will be raised
up: under God's rule he assumes the position formerly held
by the oppressor. This was the theme of Hannah's song (1 Sam.
2:8) and the psalms of Israel testify to the same thing (Ps.
113:7-8).

36:8-15 BY CHASTENING THEM GOD BRINGS THE
HAUGHTY TO REPENTANCE

There are people, however, who have to undergo a period of
oppression and humiliation for good reason. It is not in my
mind to say that the rascally man of power had the right to
treat them thus, but I do claim that God was right to plunge

them for a time into anguish and distress, even into slavery. By these means he leads them to reconsider their previous way of life. When everything goes well in our lives we neglect to examine ourselves: we consider our prosperous condition a matter of course. But during imprisonment and in slavery a person asks himself: Was there no reason why this lot has come over me? Have I always acted rightly? Did I not, in pride, elevate myself above other people, treat them unjustly, and so did I not transgress God's laws?

So, by the suffering that is inflicted by unrighteous men of power, God makes a person ready and willing to listen to his laws, and anxious not to fall back into his old errors. He slowly becomes aware that this is the reason why God has tolerated the injustice done to him. Then, when he submits himself obediently to God's punishment, that purpose has been reached; he has become a better person and may look for a better life. He then spends the years still left to him in prosperity and joy.

But the person who is deaf to the voice of God, which comes to him through his humiliating experience, can only expect more misery. By not accepting the suffering God has dealt out to him he must expect a violent death and will die without understanding why this fate should strike him. By the hardening of his heart, his unwillingness to accept suffering and to come to repentance, he accumulates an ever-growing debt with God: God's judgment and wrath become all the heavier. There is no end to his imprisonment as long as he is alive. He dies in slavery, either under the power of a hard master or as one of the temple slaves, doing the most degrading and distasteful work in the sanctuary.

That, then, is their own fault, for God's intent in permitting the misfortune that is inflicted on them is precisely to bring them to repentance and then to bless them. The misfortune is the means in God's hand to bring them solid joys and true happiness.

36:16-23 PROSPERITY CAN ALSO BE YOUR DOWNFALL

Until recently God has blessed you. So many things could have happened all those years! But God so led you that you could escape from the jaws of all kinds of deadly danger. You were completely free to act in accordance with your own wishes; you were dependent on nobody. Our servants, when it is time to eat, bring us sheepskins or goatskins full of food and put them down on the ground in front of us so that we can set to with relish; in the same way God daily sets a magic table laden with the richest foods in front of you, for all blessing comes from above. Because of your position in the community, and your wealth, which makes independence of judgment possible, you were chosen by the community as one of the judges. Anyone who looked for a fair judgment in his dispute with others sought you out.

But beware! Such a privileged position has its own dangers. I must give a warning—perhaps not to you in the first place, for in your present state no one will go to you for judicial pronouncements—but to everyone who came to be so prosperous that he was chosen to a judgeship. Let him be careful not to be drawn from the path of justice by the gifts that parties to a lawsuit want to shower on a judge. It is plain that rich people have more to offer than poor ones but it is precisely the duty of the judge to protect the poor and therefore to pay no attention to the treasures offered him. For otherwise a judge himself incurs guilt before God, and against his judgment nothing helps—neither noble birth, nor status, nor great effort.

So let not the judge, not even in his dreams, for a moment foster the fantasy of moving entire groups of people, who are in debt to some rich man, from their ancestral possessions, so that the rich man can add them to his own lands (cf. Isa. 5:8)! Let him offer resistance and not prefer the applause of the mighty to the rights of the oppressed! Just between us, Job, can you honestly say that in the days of your prosperity you never succumbed to such a temptation? When God, who is almighty, intervenes, you have to deal with an opponent who has no equal either on earth or in heaven. He acts on his own authority and no one can call him to account. Nor can you, Job, say to God: "You are acting unjustly" and ask for redress. You have gotten into that very situation, Job, and the best you can do is submit!

36:24-33 REMEMBER: GOD'S GOVERNMENT IS UNSEARCHABLE

Just as Joshua summoned Achan to give glory to the Lord, an act that implied the acknowledgment of his own sin (Josh.

7:19), so I am now asking you also to praise God's mode of conduct—in the midst of your affliction—as righteous, and to express your agreement with the doxologies that have been raised to his glory throughout the ages. One can sing of God's glory despite, or precisely because of, his incomprehensibility. All of humankind repeatedly stands in awe of it and wonders at his doings, without claiming to be able to control them. His omnipotence far surpasses our powers of comprehension and, besides that, he is not, like people, limited in his life's duration: he was and is and remains who he is, from everlasting to everlasting.

Take a simple thing like rain. When God lets the upper layer of the water ascend as vapor and then allows the vapor to condense into rain, so that drops of it come down on us from the clouds, does anyone understand, then, how those strands of haziness consolidate into cloud banks, and why this process is accompanied by thunderings in God's pavilion, the sky? At immeasurable heights above the clouds he hurls his lightning about him, and at the same time, in the depths below, he fills the water basins anew with rain so that the sea does not dry up and its bottom remains covered. Thanks be to God! For rain is indispensable to our agricultural enterprises. But let us then also praise God for his lightning, which he hurls away like spears from both hands: they strike the targets he has set for them. Claps of thunder are proofs of his irresistible power and even the raging, roaring gales have been created by him. Both that which we receive with gratitude and that which we tremblingly fear: it is all his work.

37:1-13 CONSIDER GOD'S GREATNESS IN NATURE

Such thunderstorms cause palpitations in everyone, myself included; I can feel my heart pound in my chest. How God's voice booms in the rolling peals of thunder, and how man shudders when he hears those growling sounds come menacingly toward him! That mighty hubbub is heard throughout the heavens and lightning shoots out as far as the eye can see. Those flashes of lightning are immediately followed by the thunder that causes us to tremble at the majesty of God's voice, which does not, however, restrain the lightning or call it back from its jagged course. To what end, then, does he raise his voice with such awesome effect? We do not know, it is all very marvelous, overwhelming, and incomprehensible to the human mind.

We do not know how God brings about all the effects. It appears to be enough for him to issue orders, saying to the snow: "Come down!" and the snow descends to the earth. Or to the rain, and droplets fall from mighty reserves in the reservoirs of the sky. Then there is nothing left for us human beings to do in the field; God seals up our hands, so to speak, by the mighty downpour, so that we cannot do a thing on our land and fields. For us his creatures that experience teaches us to bow down before his greatness. This also applies to the animals: they seek out a place of shelter from the downpour or hide in their dens if they have them.

Where, in the wintertime, does the cold come from? It would seem that God has his own supplyrooms for it. You yourself have spoken of "the chambers of the south" (9:9), Job, constellations we do not see in winter, so there is also a constellation in the north that comes out in wintertime. In summer the cold winds sleep in those regions, but in wintertime they leave those chambers and sweep over the earth. Soon those stars appear that we call the "Scattering Ones" and then it begins to freeze. We must not forget it is all the work of God, and so we can say that his breath turns water into ice, which, like a metal mirror, reflects the daylight.

To return again to the thunderstorms: before our mind's eye impenetrable banks of cloud come sailing by. God's lightning shoots holes into them and by God's direction they go where he wants them to and fulfill his command, however far he sends them out. This may be for judgment; who is not afraid of lightning? It may also be a blessing, for after the lightning comes the rain on which we farmers depend. The same divine power brings bane to one and blessing to another. We cannot tell God how he should distribute the signs of his favor and disfavor, can we?

37:14-24 GOD'S WORK FAR EXCEEDS OUR POWERS OF COMPREHENSION

Do not always occupy yourself just with your own lot, Job! All this that I have described to you must prove to you that

God's work far surpasses human comprehension. You have not any more than I, sat in on God's council meetings and do not know what God has instructed the powers of nature to do. Or do you know perhaps how God can make such white-hot flashes of lightning come shooting out of a dark cloud? Can you tell how God can let a cloud bank, heavy with incalculable amounts of water, float high in the sky? God does it with his perfect knowledge, which turns that which is incomprehensible to us into a reality.

When in September the weather becomes unbearably hot and the gentle whistling of the sirocco brings in the heat of the desert so that we dare not move, will you then see to it that the first refreshing rains come down? Your clothes cling to your body, and will you then, as a muscular workman, join God in condensing the mists and in stamping them into a cloud cover that can bring us water, strong and firm as sheet metal? God does all these things alone, without asking for help from anyone. Shall we then knock on his door and offer him our wonderful advice? God's work is so mysterious to us that we cannot possibly disturb him with our suggestions: "Bring down rain!" or "Hold back the lightning!" No one needs to report to him what I am saying; he does not need our suggestions.

One moment the earth is darkened by huge black clouds and there is nothing we can do about it; the next, but at God's command, the wind suddenly blows the clouds apart so that the sun can shine on the earth. Then, before the sun is even visible to us because of the clouds, we see a golden splendor appear out of the north. Like the psalmist we say: "He wraps himself in light as with a garment" and "You are clothed with splendor and majesty" (Ps. 104:1-2; NIV), a splendor and majesty before which we humans bow down in trembling and awe. In short: we human beings can never catch the Almighty in any kind of shortcoming. By his power he can do whatever in his justice he decides. Judgment, like lightning, strikes him who deserves punishment; but he does not put down those who work hard for righteousness. Therefore all men revere him. He performs his work in holy isolation, and that without asking people, however knowledgeable they may be, for advice.

THE FIRST DIVINE DISCOURSE AND JOB'S REPLY 38:1–39:38

In a sense this first divine discourse (and also the second, 40:10–41:25) constitutes a counterpart to Job's great oath of innocence in chapter 31. As regards their form, both belong to the process of a legal trial but occur at different places in that process. As we have seen, the oath of innocence occurs toward the end of a trial when the accused declares under oath that he is innocent of the accusations made against him. The divine discourses, at which we have now arrived, represent an earlier stage in the process: that in which the accused questions the accuser in order, on the basis of his answers, to prove the man wrong or incompetent. One cannot blame the writer of the book for bringing in an earlier feature of the legal process after the later one, as he orders his materials, for it was not his intention to present his story as a story of a legal trial; he only used various elements as they may occur in a legal process.

Not just the place but also the division of the roles differs. In his oath of innocence Job is the accused defending himself against charges his friends have fastened on him. In the divine discourse God is the accused who seeks to force his accuser to make an admission of his own incompetence.

While in the dialogues between Job and his friends and in the speeches of Elihu God is referred to with the two Hebrew terms that we usually translate as "God" or with a word we translate, for lack of anything better, as "the Almighty," here the specifically Israelite name for God is used, one which in some of the standard versions (KJV, RSV, NIV) is rendered "the Lord," just as this is the case in chapters 1 and 2 (on 12:9, see the Introduction under I.3). This is not a reason for attributing the present chapters to another poet than the one who wrote the dialogues; in that case one would have to deny to our poet also the authorship of chapters 1 and 2, as well as 42:7-17, and his work would then be a mere torso. It is worthy of note that in these discourses, also, the designation "God" is used a few times (39:3, 20; 40:4, 14). The name Lord occurs only in the prose introductions to the "Yahweh-discourses" and in Job's replies to them (38:1; 39:34-36; 40:1; 42:1). The first two chapters of the book and 42:7-17 are similarly written in prose form, although 1:21 approximates the form of Hebrew poetry. It would appear, therefore, that the author did not wish to use the real divine name "Lord" in poetry—we dare not say why not.

In the first discourse of God, which we are now examining, we can discern a certain systematic structure. The first five groups of questions concern cosmic phenomena; the second five, wild animals on earth. In the first five questions (chap. 38) there is reference to things that, in time and space, lie way beyond Job's reach; in the second God fixes Job's attention on things he can see in his own surroundings (chap. 39). The groups themselves are unequal in length. We present the following outline:

38:2-11	Were you present at the creation?
38:12-15	Do you arrange for the dawn after darkness?
38:16-21	Have you surveyed the cosmos?
38:22-30	Do you regulate the seasons?
38:31-38*	Do you control the powers of heaven?
39:1-7	Do you take care of the wild animals?
39:8-15	Do you employ the wild donkey and the buffalo?
39:16-21	Do you understand the life of the ostrich?
39:22-28	Did you give the horse his strength?
39:29-33	Do you determine the way the hawk and the eagle live?
39:34-38	God's challenge and Job's reply.

38:2-11 WERE YOU PRESENT AT THE CREATION?

You have repeatedly expressed the wish, Job, to have a personal interview with me (9:33-35; 10:2; 13:3; 31:35-37). Well: here I am. Just as I once spoke to my people out of a thunderstorm (Exod. 19:16; 20:18), so I now speak to you. You have spoken *of* me and *to* me; now it is my privilege to speak, not to flatter you, but to answer your accusations.

In the first place, who or what are you that you should imagine that you can tell me how I should run the world? You have no idea, nor can you understand a thing, of my purpose and plan for the world. Your own words are proof that you

*From 38:38 to the end of chapter 41 the author follows a variant verse numbering.—*Trans.*

are lacking—as everyone else is—in insight into my actions and purposes. You have arrogated to yourself a judgment concerning my government of the world and showed yourself quite the man doing it. Good; let us see, then, if you can answer my questions.

Just tell me, please, how you would structure the world. Get ready: prepare yourself for action and defense if you can! Are you perhaps finding fault with me for the fact that I created the world, and for the manner in which I did so? You should have been present to witness the event, but where were you then? Do you know how things went at the time? Please tell me; you talked about it as though you were extremely well informed—but was it you who drew up the blueprints for the world, who marked off the dimensions exactly according to plan? On what solid ground were its foundations laid? Were you the architect who planted the cornerstones for that enormous structure? When I began the construction of the earth there was joy in heaven, just as you human beings have a celebration at the start of a new construction. In that dawn the stars shone brilliantly as though they were applauding my work and all the angels sang my praises. Were you there? Do you know the "how" and "why" of it all?

Of course not! You human beings can only speak in figurative language about the act of creation. Knowing that, I shall help you a little. A while ago I used the image of constructing a building but of course we can also describe the beginning of the world as a birth (cf. Ps. 90:2). So, then, let me describe the creation of the sea as a birth; for that matter, some of your neighbors picture the sea as a person. The sea gushed forth out of the womb of the primordial ocean (Gen. 1:2). When a child is born among you human beings, people will wash it, rub it, and wrap it in swaddling clothes (cf. Ezek. 16:4). Well now: who else but me performed this task for the infant sea? I wrapped it in clouds the way people put the newborn child in diapers to protect it. But Sea was a huge and restless child: it was necessary from the start to set limits for it and to enclose it by beaches and coastal mountains, protecting the earth the way a city portal is protected by solid gates and heavy bars. My irresistible command saw to it that the floods could rise no higher than I had determined. Did you have any part in these great enterprises? If not, then why do you insist that all this should have been managed your way?

38:12-15 DO YOU ARRANGE FOR THE DAWN AFTER DARKNESS?

In a sense the miracle of creation is repeated every morning. Did you ever make the morning come? Have you decided where the dawn's early light should appear on the horizon? The earth's surface is then like a cloth from which all that is dark and dirty is wiped off or shaken out—including the "skunks," people who commit their ugly practices under cover of darkness (cf. 24:13-17), and now take to their heels. Before the first rays of light appear, at least to the eyes of men, the world is a mass of grey; but now one begins to discern outlines, like clay on which a seal is pressed, and soon one begins to see all kinds of vegetation, the living green carpet covering the earth (cf. Ps. 65:14). But the evildoers of a moment ago, the people who shun the light—well, for them no light will shine and the light of life is denied them. Their arm upraised in threat is broken; their plans are doomed to fail.

38:16-21 HAVE YOU SURVEYED THE COSMOS?

You were not present at the creation, Job, nor can you say that you have a comprehensive view of the universe as it now operates—and yet, that would be necessary before you start criticizing the way I rule the world. You have not explored the depths of the sea; all that is stored up down there remains hidden for you. Did you or anyone else—whatever fantasies may be abroad among Gentiles—ever penetrate the realm of the dead? Have you ever even seen its gates? No? Then what is the use of your talking about that dark domain?

And what do you know of the visible world? Broad are its expanses, stretching beyond all horizons, and it is full of marvels before which your limited insight must stop. Do you know where light and darkness come from, so that you could send them to their respective homes in turn to make way for each other? Still, you act as if none of this were a mystery to you; as if from the beginning of the creation (cf. Gen. 1:3-5) you had been present and had had a hand in it!

143

38:22-30 DO YOU REGULATE THE SEASONS?

Do you know where I have stored up the snow to let it come down on earth at the proper time? And have you ever seen the storehouses of the hail that I sometimes use to destroy my enemies (cf. Exod. 9:13-33; Josh. 10:11; Isa. 28:17-19; 30:30; Ezek. 13:11-13; 38:22)? Do you determine the directions in which the lightning flashes? Do you know how it is that the strong east wind, the withering sirocco, blows its way over the lands? Do you punch holes in the cloud cover as channels for rain showers to come through on their way to the earth? Do you set the course for thunderstorms? Perhaps you would only let rain come down on the cultivated parts of the earth, but in my world-rule I have to take account of more than the needs of people. If it pleases me I let it rain on desolate areas where no human being lives, and clothe the wasteland in fresh green for desert animals to eat, for I also take care of them.

You and I know that Gentiles believe all kinds of natural phenomena to be gods; they talk about the rain god, himself the son of another god, and the father of the goddess "Dew"— but all that is human fantasy. But do you have a better understanding of the origins of rain and dew, how they come into being and what the background is of such fitful phenomena? Is there perhaps a goddess who gives birth to winter cold and hoarfrost? That is nonsense, of course, but have you any idea why and to what purpose I send these two from time to time? How strange and how incomprehensible it is to you that the surface of water then turns into a layer of ice as hard as rock! What is that for? Certainly not for the benefit of you and your peers? You must not think that the rotation of the seasons occurs only for your benefit!

38:31-38 DO YOU CONTROL THE POWERS OF HEAVEN?

Just look at the starry heavens! Was it your doing that the different stars of the Pleiades form a cluster that makes it seem as if they are bound snugly together by invisible ties? And consider for a moment the giant constellation Orion! How far apart its stars are from each other, the precise opposite of what you observed in the Pleiades. Was it your idea to place them at such a distance from each other, as though they were oxen freed from their harness, each of them foraging on his own in the heavenly pasture? Of course you are familiar with the zodiac and you know that some of its signs do not appear on the horizon till the middle of the summer, as, for instance, Leo with its attendant clusters. But why should that be? Do you lead the constellations on their accustomed ways, first up and then down again? It was I who set down the rules for them, and took care that their appearance and disappearance should correspond with the cycle of the seasons on earth. Were you involved in these regulations? Did you have a hand in making the rules?

The appearance of certain constellations heralds the arrival of the rainy season, but do you have the authority to tell the clouds to let down their burdens of rain? It is by my voice of thunder, not by your feeble cries, cries that do not even reach the clouds, that this happens. Are the bolts of lightning your servants (cf. Ps. 104:4), always ready to report to you for their assignments? Do you inspect the clouds before they take their designated course as though they were living, thinking beings? Do you decide how many there should be at any given moment and do you see to it that they will pour out the rain on time, like waterskins that are tipped over? And all this just when it is needed: when the drought and the heat of the sun have made the crust of the earth hard as metal and the clods cannot be pulverized—at least not by the hands of man. It is my work to soften them with showers (cf. Ps. 65:10).

39:1-7 DO YOU TAKE CARE OF THE WILD ANIMALS?

Wild animals are just that to you: wild animals; but I take care of them as well as you take care of your sheep and your goats. It is by my provision that a lion family goes out in search of prey, the father to scare up antelopes and the mother with her cubs to catch them from their ambush. Did you ever devote a single caring thought to the young ravens in their nest when they cry out hungrily to me for food? Look how they stretch out their necks, their beaks wide open and lifted high, but then the mother arrives with a piece of carrion and they are satisfied. Is that your doing? No—it is I who arrange it.

Or look at the gazelles, the mountain goats, the deer! You know approximately at what time of the year they have their young but you do not know the exact time when each mother gives birth. You do not count off the months of her pregnancy and do not determine the moment of birth. The time for giving birth arrives and the young come forth without help from man. After a short time they grow large enough to make it on their own and they go out to forage for themselves.

39:8-15 DO YOU EMPLOY THE WILD DONKEY AND THE BUFFALO?

You do provide somewhat for your domestic donkeys but the untamed ones out in the wilds—have they even been of any concern to you? Just ask yourself the question: Who gave this animal its freedom and cut it loose from any human ties? I see to it that the wild donkey can live even in desolate areas where no human food can grow, like the salt flats. The animal loves the solitude and scorns the noise people make in the inhabited parts of the world. The drivers' shouts, by which its domesticated cousins are directed, mean nothing to it. This animal is free and inhabits inaccessible mountain country, eating just any green thing. It is of absolutely no use to you—but must the worth of my creation be measured by its usefulness to man?

We can ask the same question concerning the buffalo or primeval wild ox—that huge animal which is found in the marshes of the headlands of the Jordan. You cannot put it to work for you or get it near a manger in a barn. Can you put it to a plow, as you do with your domestic oxen (1:3), or make it pull a harrow over a plowed field? It would be wonderful for you if that were possible: one of these brutes has more strength than two of your oxen! It would cost you less energy too; you could leave everything to this animal, even letting it bring the heavy bundles of grain to the threshing floor in the village. But it will not do it and so it is of no use to you. Does this mean that this enormous beast is of no value whatever? Perhaps not to you, but it is to me; I take great pleasure in it.

39:16-21 DO YOU UNDERSTAND THE LIFE OF THE OSTRICH?

Look at the ostrich in the grassland! How excitedly she flaps her wings! But however widely she spreads them, she cannot raise herself into the air. She is much larger than a stork or a hawk but they can fly, as she cannot. For that reason she cannot build her nest in the treetops or high on a crag, and is forced to lay her eggs in the sand and hatch them there, without worrying about the possibility that some wild beast may trample them. You get the impression that she cares very little for her young, which, as a result, soon go their own way. When a predator attacks them, all the effort of laying the eggs and hatching them is for nothing, but it does not seem to concern the ostrich mother. I have not given her the capacity to develop what little brains she has. But when she rises from her kneeling posture over her eggs and pushes herself away from those horny toes of hers, she soon reaches a speed with which no one on horseback can compete. A strange animal, the ostrich, but there is no danger that it will die out!

39:22-28 DID YOU GIVE THE HORSE ITS STRENGTH?

As a peace-loving grain grower and dairy farmer you have never had to deal with horses; it is an animal for the armed forces. But you must have seen an armed contingent of men on horseback go past and been astonished over the speed of horses whose manes flowed up wavingly in the wind. They galloped in leaps as though they were gigantic locusts; the head of a locust, for that matter, makes you think of a horse's head. But peculiar to the horse is that loud snorting that makes clouds come out of its nostrils. It impatiently paws the ground and quivers to be allowed to leap forward; its hooves throw up a cloud of dust.

Sometime you should see a charge of the cavalry! The enemy waits for it behind armor and shields, but the horses leap forward without fear and not even the threatening glitter of drawn swords makes them pull off to the side. The clatter of the riders' gear and weapons does not frighten them; heavier than those sounds is the thud of the horses' hooves. When in seconds the initial objective is reached a trumpet sound signals that the attack must be continued. At every signal the horse whinnies as if to say: "Haw! Another attack!" It is as if it delightedly catches the scent of a new clash from afar, and enjoys the shouted orders and war whoops of its rider.

At the thought of that mighty spectacle I allowed myself some liberties but now I return to what I asked you earlier: Did you make the horse like that?

39:29-33 DO YOU DETERMINE THE WAY THE HAWK AND THE EAGLE LIVE?

When the cold season is about to come the migratory birds—some kinds of hawks among them—fly south. Did you by any chance give them that wisdom? And is it at your behest that the eagle soars high into the sky till he is barely visible, and builds his nest on some inaccessible crag? With eyes ten times sharper than yours, he watches from his stronghold to see if any carrion can be found. On battlefields, where the defeated dead lie, he darts down to tear off bloody hunks of flesh for himself and his young.

39:34-38 GOD'S CHALLENGE AND JOB'S REPLY

For a moment God paused, then he resumed: Do you, who had so much to say about the way I govern, really want to start an argument with me? Then please first answer the questions I have put to you! The floor is yours!

But Job replied: I now realize I can never speak with you on a basis of equality. I am too puny and all of what I would say would be irrelevant. So I am keeping my mouth shut and cover it with my hand. It is true I have spoken a couple of times but, now that you yourself have addressed me face-to-face, I do not know what to say. I have no answer. To all your questions that began with "Who?" I have to admit the answer is you, not I; and if you ask "Did you do this or that?" I can only say: "You did, not I."

THE SECOND DIVINE DISCOURSE AND JOB'S REPLY 40:1–42:6

The second divine discourse is often regarded as a later addition. This is not a necessary assumption. Job answered God's first speech with an assertion of powerlessness (39:37-38) and gave the assurance that he would not speak again. He is overpowered by the voice out of the storm and so one could say that precisely the thing he feared (9:29-35; 13:20, 21; 23:15-17) has come to pass: namely that, if his stated wish were fulfilled and he could talk with God himself about his fate, God would so overpower him that his words would stick in his throat.

Against a torrent of questions, such as comes tumbling out of God's mouth in chapters 38 and 39, he has no defense. This does not mean, however, that by this token he is inwardly convinced of God's right and his own wrong. His silence arises from powerlessness, not from consent. Refraining from speech in the face of an overpowering Presence, one may nevertheless still cling to one's own conviction.

A second divine speech follows, therefore, which after an introductory challenge describes, with the aid of a couple of examples, how there is much in creation from which man derives no advantage, which he can only shun in fear and incomprehension, but in which God delights for reasons incomprehensible to man. From this Job can learn that the world does not hinge on him as the pivot and that in the eyes of God man is not the measure of all things. Thus God brings him to the point where he begins to bow submissively before God's unfathomable ways, submits to the Reality-beyond-Reason that is God, and takes back his charges against God (42:1-6).

The descriptions of the hippopotamus and the crocodile are obscure in several places—to us at least. The reason is partly that the scintillating imagery moves swiftly by without being worked out and constantly illumines fresh aspects with new metaphors; and partly that there are purely linguistic problems, which we sometimes (as in 41:1-3) resolve in ways other than has been done heretofore. Such details do not, however, affect the picture as a whole.

The fact that the description of the hippo is so much shorter than that of the crocodile constitutes an instance of unevenness in the second divine speech, one we find hard to explain. The first covers ten verses, the second no fewer than thirty-four. One might think that part of the description of the crocodile originally belongs to that of the hippo, 40:21-28 for instance, but we cannot be certain. So we shall leave these two accounts in their state of relative disproportion and offer the following outline of God's second speech and Job's reply:

40:2-9	God again challenges Job.
40:10-19	The hippopotamus.
40:20-28	The crocodile: not to be captured by man.
41:1-8	The crocodile: invulnerable to man.
41:9-16	The crocodile: a terror to all.

41:17-25   The crocodile: a creature without equal.
42:2-6   Job's reply to God's second challenge.

40:2-9 GOD AGAIN CHALLENGES JOB

Once more I wish to give you the opportunity, Job, to tell how you would arrange the world. Get yourself ready for action and defense if you can (cf. 38:3). You wish to act as a Court of Appeals with the authority to declare my decrees null and void, do you not? You believe it to be much more important for you to carry your point than for me to be right, do you not? Your interests are obviously of more weight to you than my good pleasure.

Pretentious claims without competence do not amount to anything. Just show us whether you can accomplish mighty deeds like the ones I perform from moment to moment! But why, my dear fellow, should we even speak of deeds? You cannot even raise your voice as I continually do in the peals of thunder. Would you sing Psalm 29 and each time you come to "the voice of the Lord" substitute "my voice, Job's" for it? But that is the kind of voice you would need if you were to act as judge and governor over the world. But then you would also have to wear the proper garments, as it befits a judge who has worldwide jurisdiction, so that people can sing of you the words that now refer to me in Psalm 93:1: "He is robed in majesty"; or in Psalm 104:1: "You are clothed with splendor and majesty." By those expressions the singers of Israel meant the thunderclouds and shafts of lightning—would you feel somewhat at ease in such a suit?

Then in high moral indignation, which strikes humans as an explosion of anger but is of a much better quality than outbursts of human temper, the judge must issue his verdicts and see to it that they are carried out. Of course, there will be the arrogant ones who will not submit to your legal pronouncements, any more than you do to mine—then you must stand by your authority and make them feel the power of the court! Then you summon before your judgment seat the folks who think they outrank others and believe they are above human law, and bring them down to the humble state of the accused. Put an immediate end to the injustice that such people do to others! Let them die a miserable death, as you said I should do (21:7-20); let them be put away in the sand, instead of in an elegant tomb (21:32-33); lock them forever in the subterranean prison of the dead!

If you can pull that off you will not only receive the praise of men but I, too, will acknowledge you to be the true judge and king, and say of you what Israel now sings of me: "His right hand and his holy arm have gotten him victory" (Ps. 98:1). Then you will be the judge and king who lets justice prevail! Would you like to try it?

40:10-19 THE HIPPOPOTAMUS

If not, then look around you in the created world and see if everything is structured in accordance with the measurements of man. Just consider that huge beast which people call the hippopotamus—a creation of mine like yourself but, really, not made for your sake! It is only an animal that feeds on grass but, unlike cattle, it will never be tamed by you. It is of no benefit to you but that does not mean it has no value for me! I love to look at it and you ought at least to marvel at it. Just notice once—for this is the part that often interests you human beings most—how the hippo contrives to raise that extraordinary weight of his when the male is about to impregnate the female! What concentrated power there is in his underbelly—what strength in those muscles! And that sexual organ itself: thick and hard like a cedar! What tendons all balled together! And that bone-system, strong as tubes of metal! No human being could ever construct anything like it; it is my masterpiece, proof of my unlimited creativity. Just look at those enormous teeth; they are like swords I have given the hippo from my arsenal, so that it can rule like a king over other animals. During the day it is usually in the water but when it comes out there is not another animal that can resist this king of beasts. Whatever vegetation grows on riverbanks it views as his by right and other animals grazing there respectfully move aside, while the hippo hardly deigns to notice them. That is where those pesky thornbushes (*Zizyphus Lotus*) grow, bearing little reddish plums. They do not bother the hippo; his thick hide is not that sensitive. Sometimes he plops down in the middle of those bushes or else in the swamp reeds. He lies down in the shade of those thornbushes or else under the wadi-willows by the edge of the water. After a heavy downpour upstream the waters overflow their banks

151

and the animals, afraid to be caught in the flood, run off. But my big baby pays no attention to it whatever. Even though the stream swells and roars like the Jordan in its upper reaches, he does not even bother to turn his back to the rushing waters but calmly lets it flow through his jaws. Only his eyes and nose are visible above the water. Just try to grab him by those eyes or that nose sometime!

40:20-28 THE CROCODILE: NOT TO BE CAPTURED BY MAN

Another mighty animal created by me profits neither you nor anyone else but nevertheless has its place in my creation, and of it, too, it was said once and for all: "Behold, it was very good" (Gen. 1:31). I call it Leviathan, but by that name I am not referring to a primordial Chaos monster that threatens creation, the Leviathan of which you, Job, spoke in your first complaint (3:8) and about which certain nations have produced so many fantasies; but simply the crocodile as in your time it lives in the Nile and also in many a stream of Canaan. Can you pull that enormous animal out of the water like a fish, with rod, line, and hook; or tie its little tongue to its bottom jaw with a belt to teach it not to bite, as people do with some other animals? When a fish is caught people run a long bulrush or thorn through the gills, to be able to carry it home with ease. Will you perhaps do that with a crocodile?

Will he, like some other animals, beg for mercy in a low or a high tone of voice, whining softly to arouse your pity? Will you be able to tame it like a dog or even a leopard, which blithely accepts its fate and serves as your faithful servant for the rest of its life, so that it seems there is a written contract between you and the animal? Will you be able to play with it as with a bird to which you have tied a string, so that you can let it fly into the air and then pull it back again? Childish amusements, you say? Then try to do it for the entertainment of the little daughters of your female slaves with a crocodile! Tie one to a string!

Enough said about children's games! Just agree to go out with a number of other grown men to capture a crocodile (if that were possible!). Can you then take the captured crocodile to the market and sell its meat by the pound? Does anyone eat the meat of crocodiles? You cannot even kill one; the harpoon or spear with which you spear fish and lift them out of the water simply bounces off the impenetrable armor of its skin. Sometimes a crocodile lies sunning on a sandy shore by the river; why do you not then walk up to it and pat it on the head as if it were your pet with the idea: "No need to fight; I have got him already!" You only need to look at it to understand: This is more than I can handle! I do not stand a chance!

41:1-8 THE CROCODILE: INVULNERABLE TO MAN

There is not a soul who would dare to prod it to resistance with a stick or a stone. Who, then, will come to me with an offer to slay the beast, just as David offered his services to Saul in the contest with Goliath (1 Sam. 17:31-37)? Believe it or not, to me the animal is valuable. No one need come to me with an offer of a certain amount of money in exchange for permission to kill a crocodile (cf. Esther 3:9). I will not sell my hunting rights; the crocodile belongs to me, not to some earth-dweller, no matter who. I take pleasure in its enormous strength and in the elegant curve of its tail and I will permit no one to attack it.

No one has even skinned a crocodile; it will be many centuries before people in their love of ostentation will make purses of crocodile hide. With a gazelle you can pull off the hide that covers its flesh; but with a crocodile it is not so easy, supposing you could find one that was dead. The crocodile has a double coat of mail: it consists of a layer of bone with a layer of horny plates superimposed. And who would venture to open its jaws? The teeth that ridge both the lower and the upper jaws are so strong and so sharp they strike terror into people. After the head comes the back of the crocodile: the scales suggest interlocking arched shields with grooves in between. Do not think, however, that with your weapons you could find a soft spot in those grooves! The shields interlock very closely; and the grooves hold the shields tightly together, just as the metal ridge holds the stone in a seal. You will not find an opening between stone and metal; that is also how closely the shields on the back of a crocodile fit together: there is no space between. There are grooves between the shields but the shields cannot be parted.

41:9-16 THE CROCODILE: A TERROR TO ALL

When it comes up after being submerged and starts to sneeze it blows drops of water into the sunlight, drops that glitter so that the effect is like fireworks. That impression is enhanced by the fact that the eyes shine like coals of fire through the water; they are the color of the dawn before the sun rises above the horizon. The vapor coming out of its nostrils makes one think of a steaming kettle on the stove, or of the vapors that rise at twilight from a swamp. The effect of its breathing is like that of bellows setting smouldering coals ablaze; it is as if a flame comes blazing from its throat. The neck of the animal is enormously strong; it is as if all that is strong resides there. All around he spreads terror; a feeling of helplessness comes over everyone who discerns the animal. Even the loose layers of flesh under its neck and belly are hard and stick together as if they were of cast metal. They do not quiver as such folds do on other animals. The animal knows nothing of fear, not to mention pity; its spirit is hard as basalt, comparable to the lower millstone on which grain is ground, usually with the aid of a softer upper millstone that is moved back and forth.

41:17-25 THE CROCODILE: A CREATURE WITHOUT EQUAL

At certain fixed times flocks of sheep or goats come to drink at the water's edge, the rams with strong horns in the lead. But when the crocodile comes darting through the water—which is all stirred up as a result—the rams, strong as they are, do not think even for a moment of defending themselves and their flocks, but instead withdraw quickly from the water's edge. Nor does the shepherd, even though he had a sword at his disposal, risk a fight with a crocodile. And assuming he could throw a javelin at the beast from a perpendicular stone wall, that would only mean the loss of a weapon. Iron or bronze spearpoints simply graze off the back shields as though they were made of straw or rotted wood. The animal pays no attention to arrows, and the slingshots that shepherd boys know how to handle so well have as much effect on a crocodile as a handful of stubble. The same is true of the heavy clubs that livestock guards carry with them as a rule, and the monster does not blink an eye at spears that come whizzing in its direction.

Perhaps people think it is vulnerable from below, in its soft underbelly. But there, too, it is protected by horny plates studded with jagged shards, so that one can see in the mud, by a trail like that of a threshing sledge, where the beast has crawled. The crocodile is an incredible swimmer, causing an enormous disturbance in the watery depths so that it looks as if the water is boiling, and it foams like fluids in a kettle in which the ointment maker mixes his materials. Its wake in the water glistens in the sun, a long streak of foam like the white hair on the head of an aged man.

In short, nowhere on earth will you find a being, man or animal, which is a match for the crocodile. It is a terror to all; but itself is afraid of nothing or no one. Some animals are ten times taller than it, but it does not avert its head in fear. Just as the hippopotamus surpasses all mammals and could therefore be called their king (40:15; [40:19]), so the crocodile is lord and master over all reptiles.*

42:2-6 JOB'S REPLY TO GOD'S SECOND CHALLENGE

I now sense, from the examples you have cited, the hippopotamus and the crocodile, that you are able to realize all your plans for your creation, however far these may go beyond human conceptions. Such animals we humans could not have conceived even in our boldest fantasies, and you have your reasons for that, even though we are totally ignorant of them. If you ask therefore, as you did in your first discourse (38:2), who would be so presumptuous as to argue over your purposes with the world, without having the necessary knowledge, I have to acknowledge: I did—in my ignorance; I did not realize that there are boundaries to what human beings can do and understand. Or if you challenge me, as you did at the beginning of your second discourse (40:2 [40:7]), to answer your questions and to give an explanation of the how and why of your creation and world government, then I can only be silent. There was a time I could speak; that was when I—and my friends—only took account of human conceptions, and spoke of your divine work and being as though it were human work and human being. It was all talk based on hearsay. But now I have been confronted with yourself. Although you wrapped yourself in a thundercloud as in a garment, in that form of concealment you did appear to me, and I did see

*The end of the author's variant verse numbering. — *Trans.*

you, and you did show yourself to me in your marvelous creation. And so everything has changed; everything I have said from within my human limitations I now recant. I repent of having spoken in haste and ignorance and, in deep respect for you, I cast myself on the ground, being myself nothing but dust and sand (cf. Gen. 18:27).

THE EPILOGUE 42:7-17

Like the prologue (1:1–2:13) and the introductions to the different speeches, the epilogue also is written in prose form. This epilogue, however, does not, to our minds, tie in closely with the prologue. What seems missing is God's triumph over the Adversary and the Adversary's admission that God was right, that in fact there are people, Job heading the list, who cling to God even when it seems that God has deserted them. One may, however, find an allusion to all this in God's pronouncement that Job's words, in distinction from those of his three friends, held up. Whereas the three friends kept saying that piety is rewarded and wickedness is punished, Job, even in his darkest times of despair, remains far from such thoughts and so proves that he had not served God for his own personal advantage. In the process he vindicates God against his Adversary.

Again, to our minds it was not necessary under the circumstances to describe how Job's remaining years were blessed by God. This addition seems almost to fall into the pattern espoused in the discourses of Eliphaz (5:17-27) and of Zophar (11:13-19). A divine smile breaks through in the idyllic description of Job's later prosperity, the same smile we detect in the words of Christ (Matt. 6:33): "But seek first his kingdom and his righteousness, and all these things [food, clothing] shall be yours as well." God is not as severely consistent as are human thinkers.

This last piece of prose divides naturally into two parts:

42:7-9   God's decision between Job and his friends.
42:10-17 Job's blessed end.

156

42:7-9 GOD'S DECISION BETWEEN JOB
AND HIS FRIENDS

Leaping over Job's humble reply, the author relates how God settles the dispute between Job and his friends. The Lord addresses Eliphaz, the first speaker, with the intent that he will pass on God's decision to his two friends. In Holy Scripture God nearly always speaks to only one person at a time. The men who were so eager to defend God against Job are now told that God is not pleased with their defense. They have tied piety and prosperity much too closely together. In his protests Job was a better champion for God than all his friends with their traditional wisdom, which, in its generality, did not apply to Job's special case.

Therefore the friends have to make an expiatory sacrifice as a sign that they have taken God's decision to heart. They are rich, and so their sacrifice has to be large, on a scale suited to kings or princes (cf. Num. 23:1; Ezek. 45:23). The sacrifice must take place in Job's presence, so as to show to people that the friends have done an injustice to God in the person of his servant Job. Furthermore, the prayer (without prayer, a sacrifice is an empty ceremony) will have to be uttered by Job. No plea has greater power and validity than that of the injured party who prays on behalf of those who have humiliated and insulted him. For the sake of Job, who continued to regard his three accusers as his friends (19:21), God will let himself be persuaded not to punish the friends for their misguided and inappropriate words. In silence and shame the three friends obey; Job, for his part, performs the intercessions without resentment and his prayer is heard.

42:10-17 JOB'S BLESSED END

The intercessions not only bring blessing to the friends but also to Job himself. A general reversal of fortune occurs, a reversal whose first sign will likely have been that Job is healed of his illness. At this point Job's male and female relatives again venture into his presence. Before this they held him to be a person who was rightly punished by God for unknown sins, and believed it to be safest to keep their distance from such a one (cf. 19:13-19). Now they once again enter his house and strengthen their ties with him by sharing in common

157

meals. They offer their sympathy to him for the misfortunes he has endured and encourage him by their presence and gifts: each one a piece of silver (of whose purchasing power we are ignorant), and each one a gold nose- or earring. Such gifts are new proofs of restored community and, moreover, constitute the foundation of Job's new riches.

These riches are twice the possessions he had earlier, as is evident from the list of his possessions in livestock, compared with 1:3. But all these possessions would not mean much to Job if he had not one to bequeath them to later (cf. Eccles. 4:8). To complete his happiness God gave him the same number of children as before (cf. 1:2). Is that adequate compensation for the loss of the children he had before? For the ancients, who were realistic and quite objective in such matters, it was. With a hint of a smile the author tells us the names of the daughters—the sons remain nameless. The daughters are called "Turtledove," "Cinnamon" (perfume derived from the blossoms of the cinnamon tree, cf. Ps. 45:8), and "Jar of Eye Shadow" (a little jar in the form of a horn in which the black antimony for painting the eyebrows was kept).

The three names, each in its own way, suggest the attractiveness of these girls whose beauty is now expressly lauded. The extent of Job's wealth comes out again in the fact that he could leave to each of his daughters a legacy as large as that of each of his sons; it also shows how happy he was with them. Like the patriarchs he also reaches an exceptionally old age; after the time of affliction, double the normal age set at seventy in Psalm 90:10. It is given him to see his great-grandchildren and his death is like the deaths of Abraham (Gen. 25:8) and Isaac (Gen. 35:29). In this, at least, Eliphaz is proven right (5:26)! The smile continues to the end; and we really do not need the addition of the ancient Greek translation: "It is written, however, that he will rise again with those whom the Lord raises up."

POSTSCRIPT: THE BOOK OF JOB AND THE NEW TESTAMENT

The addition following the last verse of the book noted above takes us into the atmosphere of the intertestamentary era, when belief in a resurrection of the righteous grew. This belief is seldom mentioned in the Old Testament but all the more in the New. One must not look for it in the Book of Job as it stands; it would give a totally different twist to the problem of man's lot. The issue in Job, as the poet wrote it, is the meaning of suffering and happiness, ill fortune and good fortune, here on earth.

For that reason the post–New Testament reader of Job, as he (or she) goes through it, will often sense that he is here in a world that is strange to him. Still, one can make connections, or perceive links, between this book and the books of the New Covenant. In making that statement we do not have in mind a christological interpretation of Job; in the Introduction (II.5), be it with some qualifications, we have already rejected that view. Nor are we thinking of the few quotations from Job that occur in the New Testament. We do want to refer to 5:13, quoted in 1 Corinthians 3:19; to 39:33, alluded to in Matthew 24:28 and Luke 17:37; and to 41:11, understood by Paul somewhat differently than by us. But we are more concerned about the thought-world that imbues Job and about the question whether, and how, it is reflected in the New Testament.

Along this line we discover that, just as the idea that all suffering is punishment for sin and that one can therefore reason from a person's misfortune to his misdeeds is rejected in the Book of Job, so it is repudiated in the teaching of Jesus (Luke 13:1-5; John 9:3). Paul praises the Galatians for the fact that they have not viewed his illness as proof of sin (Gal. 4:13-15) and he rejoices in his sufferings (Rom. 5:3).

Then we must refer to the joyous adoration of God's work in nature. The daily miracle of the dawn as described in 38:12-14 makes us think of the word of Christ that God causes his sun to rise upon the evil and the good (Matt. 5:45). The statement that God also causes the rain to fall on a land without people, a steppe devoid of population (38:26-27), when transposed into the moral sphere, is carried a step further in Christ's statement that God causes the rain to fall on the just and the unjust (Matt. 5:45). This also applies to the works of God that are of no practical importance to man. Examples are the hippopotamus and the crocodile in Job 40 and 41, and "the lilies of the field" (anemones and buttercups) in Matthew 6:28-30.

Above all in the Book of James we see the themes of the Book of Job continued. There is hardly a verse in this New Testament book that cannot be illustrated with passages from Job. There is, first of all, the social motif, which plays such a large role in the dialogues between Job and his friends. When there is reference in them to "scoundrels" one should immediately, as the commentary has repeatedly shown, call to mind the devious ways in which the wealthy expand their possessions (cf. James 2:1-7; 5:1-6; also cf. Job 31:38-40 with James 5:4).

James testifies to the uncertainty of possessions and life (1:10-11; 4:13-16); and, of course, Job's history is an eloquent example of this uncertainty. When a person is struck by misfortune he must remain steadfast in his sufferings (James 1:2-4; 5:7-11). In this last-mentioned passage, Job's name is expressly referred to—something unique in the New Testament. True wisdom is a gift from God (James 1:5) and comes down from above (James 3:13-18); it is "gentle, open to reason, full of mercy." Who does not think, by way of contrast, of the merciless "wisdom" of the three friends? But when James warns his readers against the sins of the tongue (1:26; 3:1-12), we recall the words both of Job's friends and of Job himself, who often goes too far in his words and "does not keep his tongue in check." The warning against the thoughtless swearing of oaths (James 5:12) could be a critical reflection on Job's great oath of innocence (Job 31).

James's warning not to judge one's neighbor (4:11-12) could have been addressed to Job's friends. So one could also make a connection between the great value James attaches to the practice of intercession (5:14-18) and Job's intercession for his friends (Job 42:8, 10), even though the apostolic writer mentions Elijah, not Job, as an example of the effectiveness of prayer. In summary: one might suspect that the letter of James is the record of a sermon given in an early Christian church after the public reading of the Book of Job or at least of certain selections from it.

These are the clear affinities between Job and the New Testament and, even without a contrived christological interpretation of the book, Job remains of great value to the Christian church.